Humanitarianism: A Very Short Introduction

VERY SHORT INTRODUCTIONS are for anyone wanting a stimulating and accessible way into a new subject. They are written by experts, and have been translated into more than 45 different languages.

The series began in 1995, and now covers a wide variety of topics in every discipline. The VSI library currently contains over 750 volumes—a Very Short Introduction to everything from Psychology and Philosophy of Science to American History and Relativity—and continues to grow in every subject area.

Very Short Introductions available now:

ABOLITIONISM Richard S. Newman
THE ABRAHAMIC RELIGIONS
    Charles L. Cohen
ACCOUNTING Christopher Nobes
ADDICTION Keith Humphreys
ADMINISTRATIVE LAW
    Stephen Thomson
ADOLESCENCE Peter K. Smith
THEODOR W. ADORNO
    Andrew Bowie
ADVERTISING Winston Fletcher
AERIAL WARFARE Frank Ledwidge
AESTHETICS Bence Nanay
AFRICAN AMERICAN HISTORY
    Jonathan Scott Holloway
AFRICAN AMERICAN RELIGION
    Eddie S. Glaude Jr.
AFRICAN HISTORY John Parker and
    Richard Rathbone
AFRICAN POLITICS Ian Taylor
AFRICAN RELIGIONS
    Jacob K. Olupona
AGEING Nancy A. Pachana
AGNOSTICISM Robin Le Poidevin
AGRICULTURE Paul Brassley and
    Richard Soffe
ALEXANDER THE GREAT
    Hugh Bowden
ALGEBRA Peter M. Higgins
AMERICAN BUSINESS HISTORY
    Walter A. Friedman
AMERICAN CULTURAL HISTORY
    Eric Avila

AMERICAN FOREIGN RELATIONS
    Andrew Preston
AMERICAN HISTORY Paul S. Boyer
AMERICAN IMMIGRATION
    David A. Gerber
AMERICAN INTELLECTUAL HISTORY
    Jennifer Ratner-Rosenhagen
THE AMERICAN JUDICIAL SYSTEM
    Charles L. Zelden
AMERICAN LEGAL HISTORY
    G. Edward White
AMERICAN MILITARY HISTORY
    Joseph T. Glatthaar
AMERICAN NAVAL HISTORY
    Craig L. Symonds
AMERICAN POETRY David Caplan
AMERICAN POLITICAL HISTORY
    Donald Critchlow
AMERICAN POLITICAL PARTIES
    AND ELECTIONS L. Sandy Maisel
AMERICAN POLITICS
    Richard M. Valelly
THE AMERICAN PRESIDENCY
    Charles O. Jones
THE AMERICAN REVOLUTION
    Robert J. Allison
AMERICAN SLAVERY
    Heather Andrea Williams
THE AMERICAN SOUTH
    Charles Reagan Wilson
THE AMERICAN WEST Stephen Aron
AMERICAN WOMEN'S HISTORY
    Susan Ware

THE ROMAN EMPIRE
Christopher Kelly
THE ROMAN REPUBLIC
David M. Gwynn
ROMANTICISM Michael Ferber
ROUSSEAU Robert Wokler
THE RULE OF LAW Aziz Z. Huq
RUSSELL A. C. Grayling
THE RUSSIAN ECONOMY
Richard Connolly
RUSSIAN HISTORY Geoffrey Hosking
RUSSIAN LITERATURE Catriona Kelly
RUSSIAN POLITICS Brian D. Taylor
THE RUSSIAN REVOLUTION
S. A. Smith
SAINTS Simon Yarrow
SAMURAI Michael Wert
SAVANNAS Peter A. Furley
SCEPTICISM Duncan Pritchard
SCHIZOPHRENIA Chris Frith and
Eve Johnstone
SCHOPENHAUER
Christopher Janaway
SCIENCE AND RELIGION
Thomas Dixon and Adam R. Shapiro
SCIENCE FICTION David Seed
THE SCIENTIFIC REVOLUTION
Lawrence M. Principe
SCOTLAND Rab Houston
SECULARISM Andrew Copson
THE SELF Marya Schechtman
SEXUAL SELECTION Marlene Zuk and
Leigh W. Simmons
SEXUALITY Véronique Mottier
WILLIAM SHAKESPEARE
Stanley Wells
SHAKESPEARE'S COMEDIES
Bart van Es
SHAKESPEARE'S SONNETS AND
POEMS Jonathan F. S. Post
SHAKESPEARE'S TRAGEDIES
Stanley Wells
GEORGE BERNARD SHAW
Christopher Wixson
MARY SHELLEY Charlotte Gordon
THE SHORT STORY Andrew Kahn
SIKHISM Eleanor Nesbitt
SILENT FILM Donna Kornhaber
THE SILK ROAD James A. Millward
SLANG Jonathon Green

SLEEP Steven W. Lockley and
Russell G. Foster
SMELL Matthew Cobb
ADAM SMITH Christopher J. Berry
SOCIAL AND CULTURAL
ANTHROPOLOGY
John Monaghan and Peter Just
SOCIALISM Michael Newman
SOCIAL PSYCHOLOGY Richard J. Crisp
SOCIAL SCIENCE Alexander Betts
SOCIAL WORK Sally Holland and
Jonathan Scourfield
SOCIOLINGUISTICS John Edwards
SOCIOLOGY Steve Bruce
SOCRATES C. C. W. Taylor
SOFT MATTER Tom McLeish
SOPHOCLES Edith Hall
SOUND Mike Goldsmith
SOUTHEAST ASIA James R. Rush
THE SOVIET UNION Stephen Lovell
THE SPANISH CIVIL WAR
Helen Graham
SPANISH LITERATURE Jo Labanyi
THE SPARTANS Andrew J. Bayliss
SPINOZA Roger Scruton
SPIRITUALITY Philip Sheldrake
SPORT Mike Cronin
STARS Andrew King
STATISTICS David J. Hand
STEM CELLS Jonathan Slack
STOICISM Brad Inwood
STRUCTURAL ENGINEERING
David Blockley
STUART BRITAIN John Morrill
SUBURBS Carl Abbott
THE SUN Philip Judge
SUPERCONDUCTIVITY
Stephen Blundell
SUPERSTITION Stuart Vyse
SURVEILLANCE David Lyon
SUSTAINABILITY Saleem Ali
SYMBIOSIS Nancy A. Moran
SYMMETRY Ian Stewart
SYNAESTHESIA Julia Simner
SYNTHETIC BIOLOGY Jamie A. Davies
SYSTEMS BIOLOGY Eberhard O. Voit
TAXATION Stephen Smith
TEETH Peter S. Ungar
TERRORISM Charles Townshend
THEATRE Marvin Carlson

Available soon:

For more information visit our website

www.oup.com/vsi/

Julia F. Irwin

HUMANITARIANISM

A Very Short Introduction

OXFORD
UNIVERSITY PRESS

Oxford University Press is a department of the University of Oxford.
It furthers the University's objective of excellence in research, scholarship,
and education by publishing worldwide. Oxford is a registered trade mark of
Oxford University Press in the UK and in certain other countries.

Published in the United States of America by Oxford University Press
198 Madison Avenue, New York, NY 10016, United States of America.

CIP data is on file at the Library of Congress.

ISBN 9780197753095

DOI: 10.1093/9780197753125.001.0001

Printed by Integrated Books International, United States of America

The manufacturer's authorized representative in the EU for product safety is
Oxford University Press España S.A. of Parque Empresarial San Fernando de Henares,
Avenida de Castilla, 2 – 28830 Madrid (www.oup.es/en or product.safety@oup.com).
OUP España S.A. also acts as importer into Spain of products made by the manufacturer.

To Steve

And to all those working to prevent and respond to humanitarian crises, locally and globally

Contents

List of illustrations

Common abbreviations

CARE	Cooperative for American Remittances to Europe (*until 1953*); Cooperative for American Relief Everywhere (*1953–1993*); Cooperative for Assistance and Relief Everywhere (*since 1993*)
FAO	Food and Agriculture Organization of the United Nations
ICRC	International Committee of the Red Cross
IFRC	International Federation of Red Cross and Red Crescent Societies (*before 1991: League of Red Cross Societies*)
LRCS	League of Red Cross Societies (*after 1991: International Federation of Red Cross and Red Crescent Societies*)
MSF	Médecins Sans Frontières
NGO	Nongovernmental organization
UN	United Nations
UNDRO	Office of the UN Disaster Relief Coordinator
UNHCR	Office of the UN High Commissioner for Refugees
UNICEF	United Nations Children's Fund (*before 1954: United Nations International Children's Emergency Fund*)
UNRRA	United Nations Relief and Rehabilitation Administration
WFP	World Food Programme
WHO	World Health Organization

Acknowledgments

In the course of writing this Very Short Introduction,
I accumulated a very long list of people to acknowledge. In
particular, I want to thank Megan Black, Gretchen Heefner, Daniel
Immerwahr, David Milne, and Steve Prince, all of whom gave
helpful feedback on drafts of this book. I am equally grateful to
the two anonymous reviewers who read my proposal and full
manuscript, offering me invaluable critiques and suggestions on
both documents. My thanks also go to Elisabeth Piller for her
comments on my original proposal, to Andrew Preston for his
sage advice on writing such a short book, and to Boyd van Dijk,
who recommended many valuable books and articles to me. At
Louisiana State University, I have immense appreciation for my
terrific colleagues, who welcomed me into their academic
community and supported this project both intellectually and
materially. At Oxford University Press, Nancy Toff encouraged this
project from the beginning, while Lucy Randall guided it through
to completion—I am fortunate to have worked with both these
outstanding editors. My thanks also extend to Imogene Haslam,
Chelsea Hogue, and the many other individuals at OUP who were
involved in the production process. Finally, I would like to
acknowledge the countless scholars, practitioners, and journalists
whose research, publications, and labors made it possible for me to
write this book. I have learned so much from all of you about
humanitarianism past and present—you have my sincere gratitude.

Chapter 1
What is humanitarianism?

In May 2016, nine thousand people from 173 nations assembled in Istanbul to attend the first-ever World Humanitarian Summit. Convened by United Nations Secretary-General Ban Ki-moon, the conference aimed to improve the international community's responses to human suffering globally. Its participants represented many diverse interests. They included governments, intergovernmental agencies, nongovernmental organizations (both faith-based and secular), businesses, and populations affected by crisis. During the two-day summit, these delegates discussed a wide range of issues, including addressing the impacts of conflict and armed violence, enforcing the international laws of war, protecting civilians and displaced persons, mitigating disasters caused by natural hazards and climate change, and upholding the dignity of aid recipients. Some focused on the best practices for delivering emergency relief or long-term recovery assistance. Others considered how to reduce need, boost resilience, and prevent crises from occurring in the first place.

Humanitarianism, as the scope of this summit suggests, encompasses a dizzying array of issues and problems. It involves many different stakeholders, who have diverse missions, agendas, and commitments. Its emphases and concerns, and even its very meaning, have shifted across time and place. For these reasons, humanitarianism can be a tricky concept to define. Attempting to

capture this complex notion in simple terms, Secretary-General
Ban coined a pithy slogan for the 2016 summit: "One humanity,
shared responsibility." This is a decent start. A fuller, more
satisfactory definition of humanitarianism, however, lies
somewhere between this concise catchphrase and the messy
reality it tries to convey.

Many humanitarianisms

The genesis of humanitarian sympathy and action dates back
millennia. All major world religions incorporate an ethic of
charity, promoting concern and care for fellow humans as a
foundational moral principle. Over the centuries, both religious
and sociocultural values have often inspired efforts to ameliorate
the suffering of others. Some of the earliest attempts to codify laws
of war also began in antiquity. Across ancient Babylonian, Hindu,
Islamic, Jewish, Christian, and other world societies, military and
religious leaders established rules intended to make combat itself
more humane. The development of these beliefs and practices did
not occur in a vacuum; they formed in reaction to horrific crises
throughout world history. As still-haunting events like the
destruction of Pompeii, the Crusades, or the Black Death can
attest, conflict, hunger, disease, and disaster have long produced
pain, anguish, and death on a mass scale.

Our modern conception of humanitarianism, however, arguably has
a more recent provenance, located a few hundred years in the past.
In many European countries, the related terms "humane,"
"humanity," and "humanism" (and their translations) first began
circulating during the fifteenth and sixteenth centuries.
Then, somewhere around the turn of the nineteenth century, distinct
variants of these words—"humanitarian" and "humanitarianism"—
appeared on the scene. From there, they quickly spread within
multiple languages, including French, German, Spanish, and
English. These terms initially signified compassion for the pain of
others, broadly understood. But they increasingly came to connote

1. War, famine, disaster, and other forms of suffering have always plagued human societies, but organized, cross-border efforts to relieve that suffering began relatively recently in world history.

concern for *distant* suffering, sentiments that extended beyond one's local community and national borders.

Humanitarianism was not just an invention of the West. As this term took hold across much of Europe and the Americas, comparable or equivalent constructs started to develop in other parts of the world. Specialized terms denoting human compassion beyond borders, and describing assistance to victims of disaster or conflict, arose in Arabic, Chinese, Japanese, and other major language systems during the mid- to late nineteenth century. Though the English word "humanitarianism" derives from Latin and French, efforts to capture the meaning of this concept through language were widespread.

Over the next two centuries, humanitarianism grew from an embryonic idea into a multifaceted set of beliefs, practices, and principles. Across those same decades, an identifiable international humanitarian system coalesced and evolved, becoming an integral part of interstate relations and global governance. One can now speak of a long history of humanitarian crises and humanitarian assistance, of humanitarian organizations and humanitarian movements, of humanitarian governance and humanitarian law.

Trying to ascribe some sort of universal or objective meaning to this fluid concept, many prominent players within the humanitarian system have proposed definitions of the term. In recent decades, scholars across many academic disciplines—history, political science, anthropology, legal theory, and sociology, among others—have done the same, advancing their own interpretations of humanitarianism while debating its proper parameters.

Among the most influential of these definitions are those crafted by the International Red Cross and Red Crescent Movement, the world's largest humanitarian network. Central to its institutional mission are the goals "to prevent and alleviate human suffering" and "to protect life and health . . . in particular in times of armed conflict and other emergencies." Officially guiding its pursuits, moreover, are seven Fundamental Principles: humanity, impartiality, neutrality, independence, voluntary service, unity, and universality.

For many observers, these activities and values exemplify humanitarianism. Yet these attributes are not immutable, and they have shifted considerably over time. When the International Red Cross Movement was established in 1863, its promises of protection extended only to sick and wounded soldiers and the medical personnel who aided them. Over the next century, its sphere of activities steadily expanded to include sailors, prisoners of war, civilians, refugees, and disaster survivors. Some categories of sufferers, however, still fell outside its official remit. In addition, it was only in 1965—more than a century after its founding—that the

leaders of this global humanitarian network proclaimed all seven
Fundamental Principles and incorporated them into the
Movement's governing statutes. This influential conception of
humanitarianism, in short, has never been set in stone. It has been
subject to continual revision as historical circumstances have
changed.

The International Red Cross and Red Crescent Movement,
moreover, does not have the last word on this issue. Many other
practitioners and aid organizations have proposed their own
definitions of humanitarianism—some of them in direct
opposition to Red Cross principles. In the early 1970s, the
founders of the aid organization Médecins Sans Frontières
(Doctors Without Borders) openly rejected the Movement's rigid
adherence to the principles of neutrality and impartiality.
Humanitarians, they argued, sometimes bear a responsibility to
speak out on behalf of the vulnerable, calling attention to mass
atrocities, human rights abuses, and crimes against humanity.
According to this view, the twin duties to care and bear witness
(*soigner et témoigner*) are both essential elements of
humanitarianism.

Debates regarding the merits of neutrality and impartiality versus
advocacy and activism are only the beginning. Over the years,
practitioners and academics have struggled to agree on what sorts
of activities should properly be categorized as humanitarian.

One major question concerns humanitarianism's field of action
and its legal boundaries. The term is often associated with aid to
populations affected by conflict and armed violence, and with the
international laws of war. Yet conflict is not humanitarianism's
only domain. Providing assistance to victims of disaster, famine,
epidemics, and other peacetime crises is also widely understood as
a humanitarian activity, and many aid organizations regularly
perform these sorts of tasks. The lines between war and peace,
moreover, are not always neat and tidy. Natural hazards, food

insecurity, and infectious disease often occur in the midst of
armed conflict, greatly exacerbating human suffering. In the late
twentieth century, practitioners coined the phrase "complex
humanitarian emergencies" to describe these sorts of situations
and the challenging terrain on which aid workers operate. Still,
the blurriness between these spheres can make it difficult to
determine what counts as a legitimate humanitarian space.

Another key area of debate pertains to time scale. Some
definitions classify humanitarian action as the delivery of
short-term, emergency relief. Humanitarian aid, according to this
view, is designed to save lives and ensure that a population's basic
needs—for food, water, clothing, shelter, and acute medical
care—are met during times of crisis. Borrowing from German
poet Bertolt Brecht, the journalist David Rieff summarized this
approach as providing "a bed for the night." Critics of this model,
however, view it as too limited. Humanitarianism, they contend,
entails more than alleviating immediate suffering. It should also
include longer-term recovery and reconstruction assistance,
lasting well after a humanitarian crisis has occurred. Additionally,
such critics suggest, it ought to involve efforts to mitigate and
prepare for the risks of war and disaster before they ever occur, by
developing local capabilities, reducing vulnerability, and
promoting peace. As these disagreements reveal, deciding when
humanitarian action truly begins and ends can pose a challenging
intellectual and practical exercise.

A third point of contention concerns the appropriate relationship
between humanitarians and the populations they assist.
Humanitarians have traditionally been portrayed as individuals
with altruistic or even transcendent motivations, guided by
universal principles as they assist victims of a crisis. To be sure,
doubts about this romanticized image routinely surface. Critics
have condemned humanitarians for a wide range of offenses and
abuses, including paternalism, racism, coercion, and physical and
sexual violence toward the populations they assist. Such behaviors,

however, are often framed as merely a divergence from some archetypal humanitarian ideal.

In recent decades, an alternative model of humanitarianism, known as the "resilience paradigm," has begun to challenge this classical depiction. This approach emphasizes the capacity of local people and their communities to respond to crisis, rather than depending on external assistance and expertise. It empowers local populations by granting them the ability to determine their own material needs, cultural norms, and survival strategies. Instead of treating crises as exceptional, bounded events, the resilience paradigm treats crisis as a protracted or even permanent condition—as a new normality for many societies around the world. Although this model has not supplanted the classical understanding of humanitarians and their work, it has led to new ways of thinking about the power dynamics between aid donors and recipients, the aims of international assistance, and the very meaning of humanitarianism itself.

Yet another challenge in locating a mutually satisfactory definition of humanitarianism lies in the concept's plural nature. Many different humanitarian traditions exist in the world, rooted in diverse national, cultural, and religious contexts. One could point to numerous expressions of what are arguably humanitarian ideas and practices, both historically and in the present day. Rather than trying to bound the concept under a single definition, it is perhaps preferable, in the words of the political scientist Michael Barnett, to acknowledge "the existence of multiple humanitarianisms." Still, the task remains to determine what they all share in common and to identify what connects the world's many humanitarian traditions across time and place.

Humanitarianism and its cousins

Further frustrating attempts to make sense of humanitarianism is its close resemblance to several other concepts, such as charity and philanthropy, pacifism, human rights, and international development. Although it shares certain parallels with each of these ideas, a variety of legal, philosophical, and practical differences distinguish humanitarianism from its intellectual relatives.

Both charity and philanthropy have long been conflated with humanitarianism, for understandable reasons. All three concepts refer to voluntary acts of giving, motivated by compassion, which are intended to help the less fortunate. Throughout much of the nineteenth century, these concepts closely overlapped and were often used interchangeably. By the late 1800s, however, each had begun to take on more specific connotations, with subtle differences in meaning that hardened as the twentieth century progressed.

Humanitarianism increasingly referred to organized efforts to assist populations affected by an international emergency—most commonly war, but also disasters and displacement. Charity, meanwhile, became more associated with one-time or temporary donations of money, material aid, or labor. It tended to imply direct help to people in need, such as the poor or the ill, or support for various social causes. Philanthropy, finally, came to signify the strategic allocation of wealth in order to achieve broad social and welfare goals. In contrast to charity, philanthropy implied a longer-term investment, designed to address the root causes of social problems and to effect systemic change. Whereas charity and philanthropy applied to projects at home as well as abroad, humanitarianism assumed a more cosmopolitan essence, referring primarily to compassion that crossed national or imperial borders.

Humanitarianism is also routinely confused with pacifism, yet in fact the concepts are better understood in opposition to one another. During the nineteenth and early twentieth centuries, as humanitarian ideals first gained traction in world affairs, a transnational peace movement arose simultaneously, becoming one of the most influential social movements of its day. Although self-styled humanitarians and pacifists often traveled in similar reform circles, a fundamental ideological split divided the two camps. Pacifists renounced war. Viewing it as a cruel and outdated custom, they strove to eliminate it entirely. Just as abolitionists had destroyed the cruel institution of slavery, as the Russian author and pacifist Leo Tolstoy insisted, societies held the power to achieve "life without war." In the future, he envisioned, "there will be no wars or armies of the utterly unreasonable and immoral sort that exist today." Humanitarians, by contrast, started from the premise that armed conflicts were horrible, yet inevitable. Believing it a fool's errand to try to end war, they instead concentrated their energies on making conflict more humane. By establishing international laws of warfare, enacting protections for soldiers and civilians, outlawing certain categories of weapons, and through other similar reforms, humanitarians endeavored to civilize warfare and limit its brutality.

Humanitarians viewed these reforms as positive and progressive steps, but ardent pacifists like Tolstoy disagreed. By masking war's true horrors, they contended, humanitarianism only served to perpetuate armed conflict, recasting its violence as legally sanctioned, morally permissible, and socially palatable. Not restricted to the past, disputes over the merits and dangers of humanizing warfare have endured well into the present day, cropping up in contemporary debates over the legitimacy of drone warfare and autonomous weapons systems.

The relationship between humanitarianism and human rights is perhaps the most vexed of all. As the historian Michael Geyer observes, the two ideas share "a troubled rapport." Both concepts emerged at roughly the same time, in the late eighteenth and early nineteenth centuries, and went on to influence the conduct of modern and contemporary international relations in profound ways. Human rights and humanitarianism both stem from a shared ethical commitment to improving human welfare, yet they evolved along separate historical trajectories, diverging in their emphases, principles, tactics, politics, and philosophical and legal underpinnings. Though they developed distinct identities, humanitarianism and human rights have repeatedly converged, leading to mounting confusion over their respective boundaries.

Trying to tease out their essential differences, humanitarian organizations, human rights activists, and scholars have proposed various criteria that distinguish the two phenomena. Humanitarianism, according to these schemas, is grounded in moral sentiments, beneficence, and compassion. It prioritizes addressing people's basic needs and protecting them from bodily harm. It focuses on resolving urgent, life-or-death problems. Human rights, by contrast, is rooted in legal principles and traditions. Its primary emphasis rests in securing people's inherent entitlements to justice, citizenship, and equality. Its adherents seek to achieve enduring political and legal changes that will reduce inequities and upend traditional hierarchies. Although these binaries are imperfect, they provide a useful framework for comparing these complementary ideals.

International development is also geared toward bettering the human condition, yet like human rights, it differs from humanitarianism in several notable ways. Customarily, humanitarian aid has focused on addressing the acute symptoms of immediate suffering. It prioritizes short-term relief, intended to save lives in an emergency and to restore populations to a state of pre-crisis normalcy. Development assistance, by contrast, concentrates on the structural causes of human misery. It places an emphasis on long-term, sustainable efforts to transform a society's prevailing economic, political, social, and environmental conditions, with the goal of enhancing people's lives, livelihoods, and opportunities. If humanitarianism seeks to help people reconstruct their lives in moments of crisis, development aspires to empower societies to construct a better future.

Even as it remains possible to identify distinctions between humanitarianism and its conceptual cousins, the divides between them have never been absolute or impermeable. And while these categories have always overlapped and converged, they have become progressively more entangled since the mid-twentieth century, and even more so in recent decades. Among practitioners and within academic circles, the growing use of such terms as "rights-based humanitarianism," "humanitarian philanthropy," and "the humanitarian, development, and peace nexus" illustrates the entwined nature of these concepts in contemporary affairs. So, too, does the considerable attention devoted to the matter of "humanitarian intervention." Since the 1990s, contentious debates have raged over the legitimacy of humanitarian interventions—that is, military operations against sovereign governments accused of perpetuating crimes against humanity and violating universal rights. Deliberations over whether to invade Rwanda, Kosovo, Iraq, and other nations, avowedly to protect their populations from harm, reflect the close intersection of humanitarianism and human rights in contemporary international relations.

Humanitarianism arguably has its own historical lineage and certain essential attributes. Even so, the boundaries demarcating this concept from its intellectual relatives are often blurry and contested. They are also constantly in flux, for none of these concepts has a fixed or timeless meaning. Over the decades, the interplay between humanitarianism and its close kin—charity and pacifism, human rights and development—has shaped each of these phenomena in discernible ways. Never existing in isolation, they evolved alongside one another, in mutually constitutive relationships.

A working definition

If Ban Ki-moon's "one humanity, shared responsibility" provided a potential starting point for defining humanitarianism, the historian Emily Baughan offers another. "If there is anything that unites the diverse range of practices and principles 'humanitarianism' encompasses," Baughan concludes, "it is surely fluidity, or even ideological promiscuity."

Echoing this observation, this book concedes from the outset that there exist myriad possible ways to define humanitarianism—many of them quite compelling. And yet, for all their assorted differences, most definitions of humanitarianism converge around a common set of themes. All of them, moreover, seek to answer the same fundamental question: What *is* humanitarianism?

This book aspires to do the same. To that end, it adopts the following constellation of ideas as a capacious, working definition. Humanitarianism, in the pages that follow, encompasses a range of sentiments and organized actions that are concerned with saving lives, alleviating suffering, and maintaining human dignity. Transcending cultural, racial, national, and imperial borders—in principle, if not always in reality—these ideals and practices are oriented toward improving humanity.

But definitions and theories can only get us so far. To demonstrate how this nebulous concept actually operates, this book examines the major events and trends that have shaped humanitarianism in a global context over the past three centuries. It also traces the origins, evolution, and current state of the international humanitarian system, a worldwide network of organizations, movements, and legal structures that plays a central role in modern history and contemporary global affairs. Throughout, it considers the tensions between local humanitarian traditions and ostensibly universal humanitarian principles, as well as the ethical issues and political stakes associated with humanitarian governance. In addition to explaining what humanitarianism is, in short, this book describes how humanitarianism came to be.

Understanding humanitarianism, in all its dimensions, is key to grasping some of the most pressing problems facing the world today. According to recent United Nations estimates, hundreds of millions of people will require humanitarian assistance and protection each year, due to internal displacement, armed conflict, food insecurity, disasters, and the consequences of climate change. In the coming years, many observers anticipate, these already grim figures will only continue to worsen. The international humanitarian system, in turn, plays a powerful role in twenty-first-century global governance. The aid sector is a multibillion-dollar industry, which employs hundreds of thousands of people and exerts considerable influence in world affairs. Yet the humanitarian sector is also increasingly beleaguered. In recent years, funding cuts and soaring needs, internal and external criticisms, and a backlash against core principles, norms, and values have all prompted existential debates over humanitarianism's future. This book provides the knowledge and context essential for comprehending modern humanitarianism and engaging with these vital issues and conversations.

Chapter 2
Origin stories

Humanitarianism has no single point of origin or moment of inception. The practices, sentiments, and principles associated with this concept have dense historical roots, traceable to multiple parts of the world and stretching from antiquity to the early modern era.

Though they built on earlier precedents and precursors, the identifiable outlines of modern humanitarianism arguably began to coalesce at a later, more specific moment: between the mid-eighteenth and the mid-nineteenth centuries. Across these decades, concern for human suffering extended beyond local communities, and even national borders, to a far greater extent than ever before. At the same time, organized campaigns to relieve that misery began to multiply, giving rise to humanitarian movements that united adherents across nations, empires, and oceans. Major currents in world history—among them the Enlightenment, the Age of Revolutions, and the Industrial Revolution—created a conducive environment for these developments to occur. By the middle of the nineteenth century, these trends had laid the ideological, intellectual, and cultural foundations for more coherent structures of international humanitarianism, which took form in the decades that followed.

While it remains impossible to pinpoint a precise date or location where modern international humanitarianism began, several potential origin stories offer complementary explanations. Together, they reveal humanitarianism's diverse, complex, and global genealogy.

Global beginnings

One of those origin stories begins on November 1, 1755, when a series of powerful earthquakes occurred in the Atlantic Ocean, roughly 120 miles (200 km) off the coast of Portugal. The earthquakes, together with a tsunami and fires they triggered, laid waste to the bustling city of Lisbon. At least forty thousand of the city's residents perished, and 80 percent of its buildings were damaged or destroyed.

Earthquakes, and the disasters they spawn, were certainly nothing new or out of the ordinary. What *was* novel about this calamity was the international outpouring of concern and material aid that followed. Offers of assistance streamed in from Madrid, London, Hamburg, and elsewhere. Soon thereafter, foreign ships carrying money, food, and relief supplies began arriving in Portuguese ports. Before this point, such coordinated responses to disasters were exceedingly rare. Yet in 1755, governments and citizens of other nations came to Lisbon's assistance with great fervency.

They did so for various reasons. Some saw diplomatic value in supporting a struggling ally. Others spied an economic interest in helping the Portuguese Empire, a key trading partner, to recover. Perhaps most importantly, the largely unprecedented international response to the Great Lisbon Earthquake reflected a distinct intellectual and cultural shift, a budding revolution in humanitarian sensibilities.

Over the next century, catastrophes in other parts of the world spurred similar bursts of international concern and compassion. After an earthquake destroyed the city of Caracas, Venezuela, in 1812, the US government contributed money and supplies to survivors, acting, in Representative John C. Calhoun's words, "to aid the cause of humanity." When famine gripped Ireland during the 1840s—due to the combined effects of a potato blight and British imperial policies—aid arrived from as far afield as the Ottoman Empire, the Vatican, and British colonies in the Caribbean and South Asia. Much as they had in Lisbon, a combination of political, economic, and moral motivations guided these international relief efforts and a growing number of others like them.

While specific disasters increasingly compelled people to aid populations beyond their borders, many people also joined campaigns against institutions and social practices they deemed cruel or unjust. In the late eighteenth and early nineteenth centuries, movements to improve the lots of prisoners, widows and orphaned children, political and religious refugees, and other disadvantaged groups arose throughout Europe and North America. Their adherents forged international networks to lobby for reform, exchanging information, ideas, and tactics with one another.

Underpinning these diverse movements was a shared commitment to a common cause: the defense of humanity itself. Empathy for fellow human beings—no matter their race, gender, religion, or nationality—increasingly inspired and justified actions intended to reduce distant suffering. Yet for all its cosmopolitan idealism, this wellspring of humanitarian sentiments also exhibited some decisive limits and logical inconsistencies. Ideologies of racial, cultural, and religious superiority and inferiority imbued many avowedly humanitarian activities. Pledging to uplift weaker races, to protect women and children, or to save persecuted religious groups, powerful states began rationalizing war and empire-building as humanitarian pursuits. Locating the origins of modern humanitarianism requires reckoning with its inherent contradictions and moral ambiguities.

The international campaigns against slavery and the slave trade
epitomize the era's mass movements carried out in the name of
humanity, while also reflecting some of these broader tensions and
complexities. From the early 1500s onward, the practice of
enslaving African peoples and selling them as chattel labor in the
Americas grew deeply entrenched. Reliance on enslaved African
labor became integral to European colonial ventures throughout
the Western Hemisphere. Opposition to this brutal and
dehumanizing system had always existed—including, not least,
among enslaved people themselves. Not until the late eighteenth
century, however, did Europeans and their colonial American
descendants begin protesting slavery in significant numbers. By
the early nineteenth century, these critics had built an
intercontinental social movement, dedicated to improving human
welfare by destroying the institution of slavery.

The antislavery movement started with the more modest goal of
ending the Atlantic slave trade. Between 1807 and 1818, bowing to
intense pressure, the governments of Great Britain, the United
States, the Netherlands, Spain, and France all banned the
international sale and importation of enslaved people within their
respective empires. Having achieved these victories, activists set
their sights on abolishing slavery itself. Over the next several
decades, they saw steady progress, with governments outlawing
enslaved labor throughout most of the Americas (with a few
stubborn holdouts) by 1865.

The antislavery movement mobilized supporters by appealing to
their sense of humanity, a strategy crucial to its eventual success.
Abolitionists urged their compatriots to sympathize with enslaved
peoples, recognizing the physical suffering and emotional anguish
they experienced. Once stirred by these emotions, they must then
act "in the name of humanity which is outraged," as the
abolitionist Frederick Douglass implored, to eradicate the scourge
of slavery. Preaching these messages through pamphlets, sermons,
and broadsides, antislavery advocates convinced sufficient

numbers of white Europeans and Americans to view African peoples as fellow humans who deserved to be treated with compassion and some modicum of decency. While other factors contributed to the gradual erosion of chattel slavery in the Atlantic world, overcoming such a widespread and lucrative practice required this transformation in humanitarian sensibilities.

0 ⸻ USA.18 / Droit ⸻ 1 cm

2. During the nineteenth century, members of the transatlantic antislavery movement appealed to notions of a shared humanity to build support for their cause.

As abolitionists were marshaling the language of humanity to
condemn slavery, many of their compatriots were employing
similar rhetoric to justify imperial pursuits. Though it may sound
paradoxical to twenty-first-century ears, defenders of European
colonialism in the nineteenth century often rationalized their
conquests of foreign lands as civilizing missions, undertaken to
improve the lives and afterlives of fellow humans.

Although powerful states had colonized other parts of the world
for centuries, the tendency to define these exploits as
humanitarian projects gained currency across the first two-thirds
of the nineteenth century. From the Dutch in the East Indies, to
the French in Algeria and Indochina, to the British in India, South
Africa, and Australia, Europeans convinced themselves of the
benevolence of their imperial ventures—or claimed to, at the very
least. Fueled by contemporary racial theories, which stressed the
superiority of white Europeans over nonwhite populations, they
assumed both the duty and the right to govern supposedly
"backward" peoples in Asia, Africa, and elsewhere. By the late
nineteenth century, when colonial expansion accelerated in a
surge called the "New Imperialism," humanitarian justifications
for empire-building had become ubiquitous. This logic
underpinned not only European colonialism but also the imperial
ventures of the United States, Japan, Argentina, and other
rising powers.

Imperial humanitarianism took different forms. Viewing
Indigenous peoples as primitive and often barbaric, colonial
authorities routinely pledged to protect them from harm. British
citizens, for example, established an Aborigines' Protection
Society in 1837, intended to ensure the well-being of Indigenous
peoples throughout the British Empire. In the United States,
President Andrew Jackson defended his Indian Removal policies
in humanitarian terms as well, reasoning that Native American
peoples would die out otherwise. "Humanity and national honor,"
he declared in 1829, "demand that every effort should be made to

avert so great a calamity." Beyond vowing to protect their colonial subjects, officials also promised to civilize and modernize them—that is, to remake them in their own image. To that end, colonial officials promoted the virtues of capitalism and wage labor, introduced new technologies and consumer goods, reformed health and sanitary conditions, and undertook other welfare initiatives. Eager to rescue souls as well as bodies, they worked closely with missionary societies, whose members attempted to spread Christianity while stamping out Islam, Hinduism, and other local religions.

Imperialists may have lauded themselves for bettering the lives of fellow (albeit inferior) humans, yet for people living under colonial rule, such invocations of humanity were undercut by the paternalism, condescension, and flat-out racism of colonial officials. Language of protection and rescue rang hollow, moreover, alongside the everyday realities of colonial violence, labor exploitation, and campaigns to exterminate local cultures and traditions. Even as humanitarianism formed a key rationale for empire-building, to many colonized people it represented an empty and hypocritical promise.

In addition to buttressing imperialism, European pledges to defend humanity became a rationale for several armed conflicts and breaches of national sovereignty during the early nineteenth century, resulting in some of the world's first humanitarian interventions. In 1827, the British, French, and Russian navies together attacked the Ottoman Empire, acting in support of Greek rebels fighting for their independence. Although multiple geopolitical motives underlay this military operation, the three allies emphasized that their primary aim was to protect Greek Christians from violence and persecution. The "imperative duty of humanity," they claimed, compelled them to intervene and prevent further Greek suffering. This humanitarian justification for war was both shaky and controversial. Nevertheless, protecting Christian populations from harm became a precedent for subsequent European military incursions against the Ottoman Empire, including in Lebanon during the early 1860s and the Balkans in the late 1870s.

In West Africa, arguments for using military force to defend weaker populations intersected with the politics of antislavery and imperialism, and with prevailing ideologies of racial and cultural superiority. After becoming the first major European power to outlaw the Atlantic slave trade in 1807, the British Empire deployed Royal Navy ships to the West African coast to enforce this ban. Beginning in the 1840s, British authorities went further, using the moral justification of suppressing slavery to validate the colonization of West Africa itself. Wielding the threat of military force, British officials pressured many local rulers to cease their participation in the slave trade. Those who refused faced British naval bombardments and, in some cases, the British annexations of their kingdoms and territories. In coming decades, Britain and other European powers made the abolition of slavery a primary pretext for conquering and colonizing almost the entire African continent, insisting these interventions were undertaken in "the cause of humanity."

International disaster relief, antislavery activism, and imperial politics indelibly shaped the contours of modern humanitarianism, yet this flourishing concept was not just a product of western European empires or the North Atlantic world. Between the mid-eighteenth and mid-nineteenth centuries, events, ideas, and practices from other regions contributed additional layers to its rich and global historical lineage.

In mid-nineteenth-century Japan, for instance, physicians who trained at the premier Juntendō School of Medical Studies developed a distinct ethic and philosophy of care, grounded in the principle of *jinjutsu* (the art of practicing compassion). Defining this concept in universal terms, they argued that practitioners must deliver medical care without regard to borders, no matter a patient's ethnicity, social class, or political allegiances. From this emphasis on universal compassion arose a novel concept, *jindō* (human way), a distinctly Japanese understanding of humanitarianism. In their responses to epidemics, disasters, famine, and conflict, physicians increasingly put these ideals into practice. By the 1860s, they had laid a firm intellectual foundation for Japanese involvement in broader, international humanitarian movements, which were to follow the 1868 Meiji Restoration.

In mid-nineteenth-century Mexico, meanwhile, liberal jurists were developing innovative approaches to codifying, humanizing, and enforcing the rules of war. Experiences with invading armies during the Mexican-American War (1846–48) and the French Intervention (1862–67), together with decades of internal civil conflict, convinced Mexico's Reformist political leaders to enact these new legal measures. They sought to shield civilians, prisoners of war, and the wounded from violence and to punish those who transgressed these norms. After years of deliberations, liberal politicians officially criminalized "violations of the duties of humanity" within the 1871 Mexican Criminal Code. With this act, they contributed to shaping the modern origins of international humanitarian law.

Across many colonized societies throughout the world, meanwhile, local traditions of charity and altruism intermixed with imported concepts of humanity and imposed systems of humanitarian governance, resulting in hybridized forms of emergency aid. On the Indian subcontinent, for example, severe famines occurred in 1783–84, 1791–92, 1803–4, and 1837–38, during (and in part because of) the British East India Company's rule. Despite budding pledges to protect colonial subjects, the British government did little to respond to the first three crises and provided only limited relief during the fourth. In the absence of much external assistance, local forms of mutual aid, cooperation, and charity—rooted in Hindu and Muslim traditions of philanthropy and service—remained essential to local survival during these crises. As the British Empire tightened its control over India from 1858 on, these Indigenous practices and philosophies blended with British models of voluntary association, organized social service, and Christian missionary charity. The result was a hybrid approach to humanitarian relief, which shaped both local and imperial responses to future famines under the British Raj.

While numerous other examples exist, the point is that modern humanitarianism has no single lineage. It is best understood, instead, as the convergence of multiple humanitarian traditions. Ideas and practices from many different parts of the world contributed to its intellectual and material origins, coming together to forge its multifaceted shape. Contradictions and limitations, rooted in beliefs about racial, religious, and cultural exceptionalism, surfaced from the beginning. For all its positive attributes and potential, humanitarianism emerged as an imperfect ideal.

Causes and contexts

Between the mid-eighteenth and the mid-nineteenth centuries, concern for distant human suffering—and efforts to ameliorate it—became an increasingly global phenomenon. But what accounts for the revolution in humanitarian sensibilities during this era, a development that touched so many parts of the world at once?

Material factors provide part of the explanation. Across these decades, the world grew more interconnected than ever before. New technologies, including telegraphs, steam-powered ships, and rail travel, sped up communication and travel times, making even vast distances feel much smaller. These developments fueled migration, global trade, colonialism, and missionary activity, bringing more and more people into contact with one another. In the process, different regional expressions of charity and concepts of humanity intersected, growing increasingly entwined. News of global conflicts and disasters traveled more quickly as well. As awareness of foreign crises grew, it helped foster feelings of sympathy with suffering peoples abroad. Sometimes, it spurred action to relieve that suffering, too.

Prevailing intellectual and cultural currents further contributed to the advent of modern humanitarianism. Enlightenment philosophy, influential across Europe and beyond during the eighteenth century, provided one important foundation. Enlightenment thinkers emphasized that humans possessed the power to improve their own conditions. Other key principles included tolerance, cosmopolitanism, anti-cruelty, and a belief in universal rights. Together, these ideas informed novel worldviews, fostering a sense of common humanity, greater empathy toward others, and a belief that social progress was attainable.

Starting in the late eighteenth and early nineteenth centuries, a series of transformative political and economic shifts—commonly referred to as the Age of Revolutions and the Industrial Revolution—combined with Enlightenment ideals to inspire far-reaching movements for social reform. Around the world, people decried the inequities, moral hazards, and physical debasement they associated with capitalism, industrialization, and urbanization. At the same time, many condemned the dehumanizing impacts of slavery, colonialism, and international conflict. Spurred by a heightened sense of social consciousness, these critics called for wholesale change.

Reformers tested different strategies to achieve their goals. Some embraced a more secular approach, working through political and legal channels to improve the human condition or fighting to dismantle cruel and unjust institutions. Yet for many, if not most, reformers in these years, religion served as both a primary motivation and a crucial vehicle for social change. Religious reform movements arose across the early nineteenth-century world, from the Brahmo Samaj movement in Bengal to Islamic jihadism in West Africa, from the Tenrikyō movement in Japan to the Second Great Awakening in the United States and Europe. Though they differed in many respects, each of these movements shared a commitment, rooted in faith, to improving the human condition in some way.

Modern humanitarianism arose out of these broader religious reform traditions and the moral sensibilities associated with them. Indeed, one cannot fully comprehend such foundational events as the international antislavery movement, global empire-building, or the rise of humanitarian interventions without acknowledging the religious discourses and motivations that buttressed them. Practitioners of many faiths understood these campaigns and crusades as fundamentally humanitarian in character, viewing their involvement as a sincere expression of deeply held spiritual commitments. In religion, people found inspiration, legitimacy, and meaning for their missions to better the lives of others.

By the middle of the nineteenth century, these material, intellectual, and cultural developments had made humanitarianism into a worldwide phenomenon. To be sure, local populations continued to exert their own influence on imported forms of aid and philosophies of charity, shaping them in accordance with their own traditions, values, needs, and desires. Even so, as societies and their ideas intermixed, new visions and understandings of international humanitarianism came steadily into focus.

Although the precise origins of modern humanitarianism may be difficult to pin down, at least one thing is certain: it was very much a human creation, the product of distinct moment in world history. Between the mid-eighteenth and the mid-nineteenth centuries, the identifiable contours of this concept first took hold, shaped by the prevailing winds of geopolitics, dominant cultural assumptions and racial attitudes, emergent technologies, and the beliefs and actions of ordinary people. From these beginnings, a more formal set of humanitarian structures and institutions started to evolve, building on these foundations in the years and decades ahead.

Chapter 3
Organizational and legal structures

For all the stories purporting to explain the origins of modern humanitarianism, there is one that gets told time and again. In June 1859, a young Swiss businessman named Henry Dunant came upon the town of Solferino, in what is now northern Italy. A bloody battle had just transpired, part of the Second Italian War for Independence. Thousands of Sardinian, French, and Austrian soldiers were dead. Tens of thousands more lay wounded on the battlefield, with little hope of receiving the urgent care they needed. Appalled by the carnage and the chaos, Dunant spent the next several days helping provide succor to the survivors. He then returned to his hometown, Geneva, and wrote a book about his moving experience.

Published in 1862, *Un Souvenir de Solférino* (*A Memory of Solferino*) described the devastation Dunant witnessed in graphic detail. But the book did more than depict the horrors of a past battle; it also outlined a vision for minimizing such suffering in future conflicts. Dunant made two related proposals. First, he urged all countries to establish national relief societies, composed of volunteer medical personnel who stood prepared to aid soldiers wounded in combat. Second, he called for an international treaty to sanction the existence of these relief societies and protect their operations during wartime.

Dunant's ideas proved highly influential. In February 1863, a prominent Genevan jurist, Gustave Moynier, led a commission to study his proposals and determine how best to accomplish them. This group, which included Dunant, laid the foundation for what became the International Committee of the Red Cross (ICRC). In October 1863, the committee brought together delegates from sixteen nations for an international conference. Issuing a series of resolutions and recommendations, attendees proclaimed the neutrality of sick and wounded soldiers and the civilian medical personnel who treated them. They also selected an emblem to identify these medical volunteers in the field: a red cross on a white background, the inversion of the Swiss flag. Finally, they endorsed the creation of volunteer relief associations attached to their country's respective militaries, the basis for the first National Red Cross Societies.

Ten months later, the Swiss government hosted a diplomatic conference in Geneva, inviting states to codify these proposals and principles in an international treaty. On August 22, 1864, representatives of twelve European governments signed the Convention for the Amelioration of the Condition of the Wounded in Armies in the Field, more commonly known as the Geneva Convention of 1864. Together, these events marked the birth of the International Red Cross and Red Crescent Movement. They also established the modern foundations of international humanitarian law, with the ICRC—a neutral, impartial, and independent institution—as its legally recognized guardian.

This tale of "Dunant's Dream," as one chronicler dubbed it, is often presented as the birth of modern humanitarianism itself. Yet if this constellation of events marked a critical turning point in humanitarianism's history, Dunant, Moynier, and their associates were by no means the only ones propelling its evolution. Their contributions were just one part of a broader process, whose development unfolded far beyond Europe.

Between the mid-nineteenth and the early twentieth centuries, an identifiable international humanitarian system first coalesced. It stemmed from ideological foundations laid during the preceding decades, institutionalizing these ideals in more formal, structured ways. The establishment and growth of humanitarian organizations and movements, together with the evolution and expansion of international humanitarian law, gave this system its shape. Across these same decades, humanitarian norms and principles began to inform global governance to an unprecedented degree. By the outbreak of the First World War in 1914, the effects of these cumulative shifts were plainly visible.

While the International Red Cross and Red Crescent Movement played a pivotal role in these developments, its contributions were neither exceptional nor uncontested. Many other individuals and groups proved highly instrumental. Concurrent with the ICRC's ongoing efforts to humanize warfare, other self-styled humanitarians wrestled with multiple international emergencies. They responded to crises stemming from conflict, as well as from natural hazards, famine, and mass atrocities. Putting deep-rooted ideals into practice, they built institutions and mass movements to alleviate both wartime and peacetime suffering. From these collective activities arose the organizational and legal structures that undergird modern humanitarianism.

Humanizing warfare

In the half-century that followed the Battle of Solferino, the quest to make war more humane became a worldwide movement. After the initial signing of the Geneva Convention in 1864, a growing number of states became adherents to the treaty. By 1867, most European governments had ratified or acceded to the Convention, and political leaders elsewhere in the world were beginning to take interest. In 1865, the Ottoman Empire became the first non-European party to the treaty. Following in its footsteps were

Iran and El Salvador (1874), Argentina and Chile (1879), the United States (1882), Japan (1886), and other states, numbering fifty-seven by 1907.

As governments acceded to the Geneva Convention, citizens within their countries began organizing National Red Cross Societies, whose mission—at least originally—was to furnish medical care to ill and wounded soldiers during wartime. By the outbreak of the First World War, Red Cross Societies could be found in most European nations and roughly twenty other countries around the world. Objecting to the use of the cross, a Christian symbol, citizens of the Ottoman Empire instead adopted the Red Crescent, an alternative emblem whose use the ICRC eventually sanctioned.

Unlike other charitable organizations, Red Cross and Red Crescent Societies were neither nongovernmental nor fully governmental entities. Occupying a unique middle ground, they served as the exclusive volunteer medical auxiliaries to their nation's militaries, a status recognized by both the ICRC and their respective governments. Per the terms of the Geneva Convention, their personnel, ambulances, and hospitals were entitled to legal protection in war zones as neutral entities.

The Geneva Convention and the International Red Cross Movement gained the support of government officials, military leaders, and ordinary citizens alike, but its promoters differed in their motives. For men like Henry Dunant and Gustave Moynier, both ardent evangelical Protestants, working to make conflict more compassionate represented an extension of their faith and charitable commitments. Christian, Muslim, and other religious convictions similarly inspired Red Cross and Red Crescent boosters in many other nations. For some, however, nonreligious ideas proved a more decisive factor. Many founders of the Japanese Red Cross Society, for instance, drew inspiration from deep-seated philosophical beliefs grounded in the principles of nature. This value system, which prized compassionate efforts by physicians to heal all human life, provided an important intellectual and ethical foundation for the Japanese Red Cross, one of the era's largest and most vibrant National Societies.

For many political and military leaders, by contrast, the choice to support these developments was often more pragmatic than idealistic. In the late nineteenth century, conflict was growing simultaneously more deadly and more unpopular. In this context, many statesmen viewed humanitarian reforms as a means to legitimize warfare and placate critics. Wartime planners spied other potential advantages. Although Red Cross and Red Crescent personnel should in theory assist any fallen soldier without regard to nationality, military commanders realized that, in practice, these volunteers would mainly supplement their own countries' military medical services. Their efforts to heal sick and wounded troops promised to expedite those soldiers' return to the battlefield. For the leaders of many non-European countries, finally, signing the Geneva Convention and joining the Red Cross Movement functioned as an act of public diplomacy. In the eyes of Argentine, Japanese, Ottoman, and other national dignitaries, embracing these humanitarian trends signaled their countries' rightful place in the club of "civilized" nations.

These disparate motivations reveal some of the profound tensions—between nationalism and internationalism, patriotism and humanism, militarism and pacifism—that steered the evolution of modern humanitarianism. Not confined to the late nineteenth and early twentieth centuries, these frictions continued to reverberate.

As they spread around the world, both the Geneva Convention and the International Red Cross and Red Crescent Movement faced repeated tests. Major conflicts, such as the Franco-Prussian War (1870–71), the Russo-Turkish War (1877–78), the Cuban War for Independence (1895–98), and the Russo-Japanese War

3. The Geneva Convention of 1864 proclaimed the neutrality of soldiers injured on the battlefield and the medical personnel who treated them. Japanese Red Cross personnel, who cared for wounded soldiers during the Russo-Japanese War (1904–5), acted in accordance with this principle of neutrality.

(1904–05), served as literal trials by combat. During these and other conflicts, the ICRC—still a very small institution—focused mainly on reminding belligerents of their obligations under the Geneva Convention. In a few cases, ICRC delegates experimented with novel tasks, such as collecting information about prisoners of war and channeling correspondence between prisoners and their families. Still, its actions in the field remained limited. The Red Cross and Red Crescent Societies of the warring nations, meanwhile, gained experience in treating wounded troops, operating ambulances and field hospitals, coordinating the repatriation of prisoners and soldiers, and other related tasks. Involvement in these wartime activities helped National Societies to build membership, funding, and national prestige.

To the chagrin of many ICRC officials observing these wars, the National Societies tended to behave less as independent, impartial entities and more as patriotic subordinates to their countries' armed forces. This development, which one historian has termed "the militarization of charity," was not the outcome the Movement's founders had envisioned. Nevertheless, as government and military leaders came to view Red Cross and Red Crescent Societies as indispensable to wartime operations, the effect was to bolster state support for the International Red Cross Movement as a whole, helping ensure its lasting success.

Rising nationalism, militarism, and imperialism ensured there was no shortage of global conflicts for the Movement to address. By the late nineteenth century, mounting concerns over the challenges of protecting medical personnel and the battlefield wounded convinced ICRC members that a revision of the Geneva Convention was needed. In 1906, at their behest, the Swiss government convened an international conference to amend the treaty, updating its terms and clarifying the obligations of its signatories. In July, representatives from more than thirty nations adopted the Geneva Convention of 1906, the first major revision to the treaty since 1864.

By this point, the law of Geneva did not stand alone; government leaders had begun implementing other legal mechanisms to regulate war. Seven years earlier, in 1899, delegates from more than two dozen states met in the Netherlands for the First Hague Peace Conference. Despite its name, this international meeting was concerned with militarism rather than pacifism. Whereas the Geneva Convention governed protections for sick and wounded soldiers, the purpose of the Hague Conference was to establish international rules governing the methods and conduct of warfare more broadly. Building on initiatives and proposals in circulation since the 1860s, delegates adopted a series of treaties and declarations to codify these laws of war, known collectively as the Hague Convention of 1899. A subsequent conference, convened eight years later, led to some minor modifications and additions, resulting in a second series of treaties known as the Hague Convention of 1907.

The Hague Conventions of 1899 and 1907 joined the Geneva Convention as cornerstones of international humanitarian law. Among other rules, the Hague Regulations stipulated humane treatment for prisoners of war and prohibited attacks on nonmilitary targets. They established certain protections for civilians and private property, prohibited some categories of weapons, and outlined terms for declaring an armistice and occupying defeated territories. In addition to affirming the existing principles of the Geneva Convention, the Hague Conventions extended their protections further, to include sailors, hospital ships, and other aspects of maritime warfare. In an effort to prevent conflicts from occurring in the first place, the 1899 Convention established a Permanent Court of Arbitration, intended to settle interstate disputes diplomatically. Yet, for the most part, the architects of Hague Conventions accepted the premise that conflict was sometimes unavoidable. Their aim was not to end armed conflict as an instrument of statecraft, but to "diminish the evils of war" while "modifying [its] severity as far as possible." Such outcomes, they concurred, promised to serve "the interests of humanity."

Alongside these state-led efforts to regulate warfare, many ordinary people around the world engaged in voluntary efforts to minimize the horrors of combat. Participating in the International Red Cross and Red Crescent Movement represented one popular avenue. By the eve of the First World War in 1914, millions of women and men in dozens of countries had become dues-paying members of their respective National Societies. Yet if the ICRC and National Societies strove to occupy a dominant position—or an outright monopoly, as some critics saw it—in the field of wartime relief, they were not the only channels available to would-be humanitarians.

Across the late nineteenth- and early twentieth-century world, a growing number of grass-roots organizations and movements, both national and transnational, arose to confront the brutality of militarism and combat. During these years, millions of people joined pacifist groups, with dreams of eradicating war altogether. Others campaigned for more limited objectives, such as disarmament and international arbitration, concentrating their energies on humanizing and minimizing conflict rather than abolishing it entirely. Nongovernmental organizations (NGOs) such as the International Arbitration League, the Japanese Society of International Law, and the International League of Women for General Disarmament became prominent advocates for these issues. They mobilized their fellow citizens and lobbied government officials to take action. These groups also directed their advocacy toward international conferences, influencing the development of the Hague Conventions and other governmental humanitarian initiatives.

Going beyond the ICRC's more limited focus on soldiers, many humanitarian organizations strove to assist all victims of conflict.

The founders of the Chinese Red Cross, in fact, established their society in 1904 with the express intent of aiding Chinese civilians in Manchuria, who were caught in the crossfire of the Russo-Japanese War. Entering the war zone under the cover of Red Cross neutrality, Chinese and foreign relief workers succeeded in delivering aid to some 250,000 noncombatants. For other aid agencies, both faith-based and secular, providing relief to refugees, war orphans and widows, and other civilians represented a core mission. The Hebrew Immigrant Aid Society, for instance, was founded in New York in 1881 to assist Jewish refugees fleeing persecution in Russia and eastern Europe. During the South African War (1899–1902), reports of widespread death and disease—particularly among white Boer women and children—fueled public outcry in Europe. In response, newly formed relief agencies like the Dutch Assistance Fund and the South African Women and Children Distress Fund, together with the British Quakers and Dutch Reformed Churches, sent money and supplies to aid these noncombatants. Precious little relief reached indigenous Black women and children in the region, however, revealing the stark limits of humanitarian sympathies.

Disasters other than war

Even as states and citizens aspired to minimize the cruelty of conflict, war was hardly the only humanitarian concern. Across the late nineteenth- and early twentieth-century world, organizations and movements arose to combat many other types of suffering caused by natural hazards, famine, and mass atrocities. Once a fairly rare occurrence, responding to global humanitarian crises became much more of an international norm during these years. Together, these peacetime activities shaped the evolving contours of international humanitarianism in crucial ways.

A wide range of actors became involved in these international relief efforts and advocacy campaigns. Religious missionaries and missionary societies played a prominent role. They called

attention to distant crises, mobilized donors in their home
countries, and distributed aid in affected areas. A flurry of new
NGOs and committees also appeared on the scene, devoted to
famine relief, combatting state-sponsored or colonial violence, and
other humanitarian causes. To an increasing and unprecedented
degree, governments and militaries began joining these nonstate
actors in responding to peacetime emergencies. Diplomats,
consuls, and colonial officials regularly assumed responsibility for
coordinating relief efforts in the places they were stationed.
Governments also routinely deployed their navies and armies
to assist other nations in times of catastrophe, relying on
the armed forces to provide material aid, manpower, and
logistical support.

Although succoring fallen troops remained their primary function,
many National Red Cross and Red Crescent Societies also began
branching out beyond the battlefield. At the second International
Red Cross Conference in 1869, delegates issued a resolution
encouraging societies to assist in public calamities other than war.
Among the earliest adopters of this peacetime mission were the
Japanese and American Red Cross Societies. Founded in 1877 and
1881, respectively, the two societies built their reputations by
responding to catastrophes caused by floods, fires, earthquakes,
tropical cyclones, and other hazards. Delivering disaster relief
soon became a core activity for many other National Societies.
So did efforts to combat infectious disease. In 1886, for instance,
the newly founded Argentine Red Cross made a name for itself
by treating patients during a cholera epidemic. In the early
twentieth century, the German Red Cross spearheaded a
national public health campaign against tuberculosis, one of the
era's leading causes of death. Its organized efforts to prevent
and treat the disease became a model that other National
Societies followed.

For these assorted humanitarian actors, famines ranked among
the era's deadliest and most disruptive crises. Triggered by a

combination of environmental hazards (such as drought, flooding, or insect plagues) and human causes (including political upheaval, economic inequality, and colonial apathy), famines killed tens of millions of people worldwide during the late nineteenth and early twentieth centuries. Among the most devastating, in terms of magnitude, were those that gripped China in 1876–79, 1906–7, and 1911–12; India in 1876–78 and 1896–97; and southeastern Africa during the late 1890s. As these emergencies unfolded, reports and graphic images of starvation and social unrest began to circulate globally, generating international concern.

The international responses to the era's major famines varied widely, and they were shaped by interstate relations, imperial dynamics, and other political, social, and economic factors. In China, the presence of sizeable foreign communities—composed of European and North American missionaries, businessmen, diplomats, and their families—proved particularly consequential. During the North China Famine of 1876–79, for instance, a group of prominent foreigners living in Shanghai established the China Famine Relief Fund. Members of this committee solicited donations from their compatriots, both in China and overseas, and supervised the distribution of money and food within the affected provinces.

During subsequent famines in China, foreign residents performed similar activities while also testing novel approaches to aid. In 1911, catastrophic flooding decimated crops in central and eastern China, leading to widespread hunger the following year. In this case, a Central China Famine Relief Committee, composed of both foreign and Chinese members, experimented with a newer method of assistance: providing relief in exchange for labor. Specifically, the committee hired Chinese men to construct ditches, canals, dikes, and other public works projects, paying them in food rations. Guided by a mixture of practical objectives, moral concerns, and racial and class prejudices, their goal was to prevent starvation and mitigate the risk of future flooding, all while claiming to discourage dependency among Chinese relief recipients. Not limited to China, labor-relief projects became commonplace in other disaster-stricken regions as well.

In India and southeastern Africa, European colonialism shaped both the course of famines and the humanitarian responses to them. The British Crown established direct rule over India in 1858 and proclaimed a protectorate in East Africa (present-day Kenya) in 1895, part of a broader process of imperial expansion. In both places, periods of severe drought coincided with the political and economic upheavals of colonialism to produce widespread crop failures. These food shortages—together with the British government's inadequate efforts to address them—resulted in several major famines in late nineteenth-century India and a great famine in central Kenya, which stretched from 1897 to 1901.

Although some foreign relief funds reached India and British East Africa during these crises, prevailing international norms held that imperial powers bore the primary responsibility for the welfare of their colonies. Indeed, Britain and other imperial powers proudly defended their colonial ventures as humanitarian enterprises. Because of this mindset, overseas aid flowed mainly through British imperial channels, with far less arriving from foreign nations. In India especially, British colonial authorities, missionaries, and charitable organizations expended considerable resources attempting to aid famine sufferers. In the 1880s, British officials also developed a series of Famine Codes, intended to systematize and improve future relief and prevention efforts. Yet despite some signs of progress over the years, their methods proved wholly insufficient, as they were incapable of addressing the scope and complexity of the problem. By the early 1900s, tens of millions of people across South Asia and British East Africa had died of starvation and malnutrition-induced diseases. In critics' eyes, these grim statistics raised grave doubts about the purportedly humanitarian character of European imperialism.

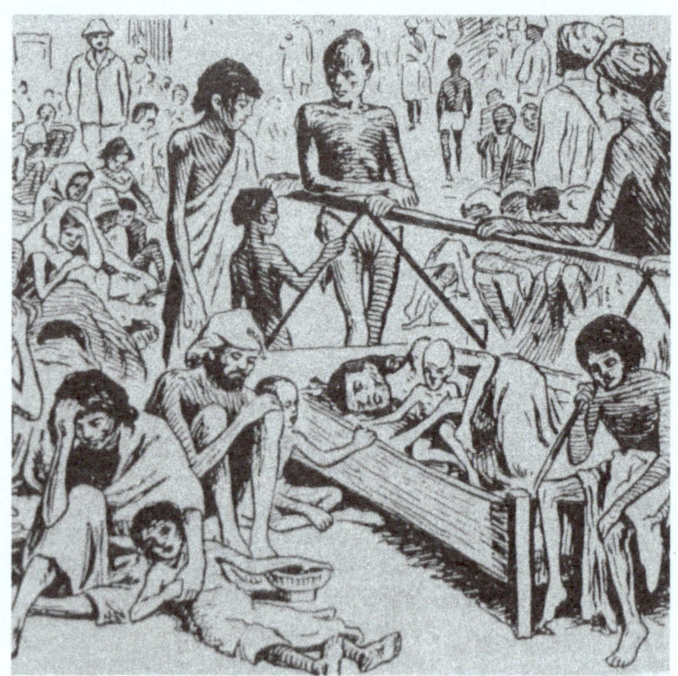

4. In nineteenth-century India, local traditions of charity and mutual aid combined with British imperial policies to shape the humanitarian response to periodic famines.

Alongside the slow, creeping specter of famine, more abrupt catastrophes caused by natural hazards—including earthquakes, floods, and tropical cyclones—became a locus of international concern during these years. One of the era's deadliest and most destructive disasters occurred in late December 1908, when a powerful earthquake and tsunami struck southern Italy. In an instant, the cities of Messina and Reggio di Calabria were reduced to ruins, leaving 100,000 people dead and hundreds of thousands homeless. This horrific crisis sparked an extraordinary international response. Multiple Red Cross and Red Crescent Societies sent money, material goods, and personnel to Italy to assist the relief effort. Russian, British, French, and US navy ships also arrived on the scene, where their crews joined the Italian military in rescuing survivors and clearing away rubble. In addition to providing food, acute medical care, and other short-term aid, several countries contributed longer-term recovery and reconstruction assistance. Most notably, the Swiss and US governments undertook major housebuilding projects in southern Italy. Sending lumber, carpenters, and cash to the devastated region, they hired Italian laborers to build thousands of cottages and other community buildings for disaster survivors.

Elsewhere in the world, other disasters prompted similar, if less sizeable, international humanitarian responses. Among them were catastrophes triggered by a powerful hurricane in Puerto Rico in 1899, volcanic eruptions in Martinique and St. Vincent in 1902, major earthquakes that leveled San Francisco and Valparaíso in 1906, a great fire in Constantinople in 1911, and destructive floods along China's Yangzi and Huai Rivers in that same year. In the aftermath of each of these crises—and many more like them—foreign governments, militaries, Red Cross and Red Crescent Societies, and ordinary citizens responded, providing various forms of humanitarian aid and rebuilding assistance. For many countries, foreign disaster relief was now a routine part of foreign relations.

While humanitarians responded to many crises deemed acts of god or nature, they also sought to redress suffering that was deliberately inflicted by people or states. In the late nineteenth century, colonial violence and abuses in the Congo Basin emerged as an international humanitarian cause-célèbre. In 1885, Belgium's King Leopold II laid claim to a vast stretch of territory in central Africa, naming it the Congo Free State. The king defended this imperial land grab as a humanitarian enterprise. In reality, it ushered in an immense humanitarian disaster. During Leopold's reign, his agents established an exploitative and violent system of labor, geared toward extracting rubber, ivory, and other valuable resources. They relied on a regime of terror to keep Congolese workers in submission, inflicting mutilations, torture, sexual assaults, and mass killings on the population.

By the early 1900s, exposés and photographs of these atrocities began circulating in Europe and the Americas, leading to mounting international criticism. Groups like the Congo Reform Association, established in Great Britain in 1904, organized mass campaigns against Leopold's rule. Protests also emanated from the emerging Pan-African movement. Addressing "the Nations of the World" at the First Pan-African Congress in 1900, the activist and intellectual W. E. B. Du Bois endorsed the Congo Free State's independence, calling for "happiness and true advancement to its black people." Eventually, these humanitarian movements achieved partial success. In 1908, Leopold agreed to transfer control of the colony to the Belgian government, which curbed some of the ruthless violence associated with his reign. Congolese independence, however, lay decades in the future.

Atrocities in the Ottoman Empire became another main target of humanitarian concern during these years. Since the early nineteenth century, European powers had frequently condemned the mistreatment of Christian minorities in Ottoman territories, occasionally using their suffering to justify military interventions. These criticisms resurfaced during the mid-1870s, when nationalist uprisings in the Balkans met with violent suppression by Ottoman troops. Reports of aggression and brutality against Christians, which included the massacre of thousands of Bulgarian civilians, sparked outrage across Europe. This mounting public ire fueled renewed debates among policymakers over the merits of militarized humanitarian interventions. In 1877, the Russian Empire ultimately declared war against its Ottoman neighbor, avowedly to protect Orthodox Christians from inhumane treatment. Yet this lofty humanitarian rhetoric also provided a convenient cover for Russia's strategic motives, namely the potential for postwar territorial gains. Focused squarely on

Christian populations, moreover, Russian and other European leaders did little to protect the region's Muslim and Jewish refugees from harm, revealing once again the selective limits of humanitarian concern.

Although this "Eastern Crisis" eventually subsided with the Ottoman Empire's 1878 defeat, which resulted in independence or greater autonomy for several Balkan territories, humanitarian concerns were far from resolved. During the 1890s, attention shifted to the Ottoman Empire's Asian interior, where Armenian Christian communities faced growing repression and persecution. Violence exploded between 1894 and 1897, when Ottoman soldiers and civilians slaughtered an estimated 100,000 Armenians, reviling them as enemies of the state. News of these massacres re-inflamed public opinion throughout Europe and North America. Concerned observers established committees for Armenian relief, which raised funds for Armenian widows and orphans and mobilized public support. Many diplomats and missionaries urged their governments to invade the Ottoman Empire, presenting humanitarian intervention as morally just. Despite this pressure, leaders of the great European powers ultimately demurred, privileging geopolitical stability over notions of humanitarian responsibility. The "Armenian Question," however, remained a leading humanitarian cause in both Europe and North America, eventually reaching a fever pitch during the First World War.

Humanitarian appeals failed to provoke international military operations in the Ottoman Empire, but in 1898 they buttressed the US government's decision to go to war with Spain. In 1895, Cuban insurrectionists began fighting for liberation from Spanish colonial rule. The humanitarian situation on the island rapidly deteriorated. Acute food shortages and infectious diseases, together with the Spanish military's brutal tactics, produced widespread suffering and rising mortality among the Cuban populace. In the United States, supporters of Cuban independence used these grim conditions to rally support for their cause. Depicting Cubans as innocent victims of Spanish cruelty and tyranny, these activists stressed that the United States had a moral obligation to intervene and protect Cubans from further misery. By 1898, their arguments had convinced much of the American public and many US policymakers that a "war for humanity" was necessary. Swayed in part by this humanitarian logic—but also by a host of other economic, strategic, and geopolitical motives—the US government declared war against Spain in April 1898, emerging as the victor less than four months later.

In the aftermath of the Spanish-American War, the US government annexed the Spanish colonies of Puerto Rico, Guam, and the Philippines and extended significant political, economic, and military control over Cuba. Eager to distance their nation from other empires, US policymakers defended their governance of these territories as benevolent in character. Their aim was to reform and uplift Spain's former colonies, US officials insisted, not exploit them. Such justifications, however, failed to persuade many skeptics, both in the United States and in its new possessions. What began as a US humanitarian intervention, in these critics' eyes, had ended with a humanitarian excuse for US imperial expansion.

Interventions in other nations—militarily or otherwise—for humanitarian purposes increased in frequency during the late nineteenth and early twentieth centuries. Alleviating global suffering, however, was not accomplished by foreign involvement alone. Local and national charitable networks continued to provide the lion's share of assistance during disasters, famines, and other crises. Local communities maintained their own customs of relief, recovery, and rebuilding. They relied on existing bonds of solidarity—among families, friends, neighbors, and coworkers—to cope when emergencies struck. As outsiders began asserting greater responsibility and authority over humanitarian crises, their actions often collided with these local traditions, needs, and desires. Competing visions about aid and protection led to repeated clashes between foreign intervenors and the intended recipients of their aid, raising complex ethical questions about international humanitarianism and its true intentions.

Relieving a world at war

By August 1914, fifty years after the signing of the 1864 Geneva Convention, the outlines of an international humanitarian system had come into focus. Though not without challenges and criticisms, humanitarian organizations and movements had taken concerted steps toward humanizing warfare and mitigating other forms of suffering. The eruption of the First World War—known to contemporaries as the Great War—tested the organizational and legal structures of humanitarianism in every conceivable way.

The Great War was a truly global conflagration. Between July and October 1914, most European powers and the Ottoman Empire became embroiled in conflict, propelled by the explosive forces of nationalism, militarism, and imperial competition. Over the next four-and-a-half years, hostilities raged across Europe, Russia, and the Near East. As Europeans descended into combat with one another, they dragged their empires in with them. Across Africa and Asia, European colonies became active theaters of war. Millions of colonized people served their empires as soldiers and essential laborers. Over time, other sovereign nations steadily joined the fray, including Japan, China, the United States, and multiple Latin American republics. This was indeed a world war.

It was also a global humanitarian crisis. More accurately, the Great War precipitated a web of interconnected humanitarian crises, affecting all corners of the world. On the fronts of battle, soldiers and sailors experienced staggering suffering. Innovations in weaponry—including rapid-fire artillery, high-explosive shells, machine guns, and poison gas—enabled militaries to kill and maim on an industrial scale. Living in overcrowded and often filthy environments, many troops fell ill from communicable diseases such as typhus, pneumonia, trench fever, and syphilis. Mental trauma, diagnosed at the time as "shell-shock," was pervasive. By the time hostilities ceased, an estimated ten million military personnel had died from battlefield injuries and illnesses, while another twenty-one million became sick or wounded. Some eight million troops were also taken prisoner and held in detention camps, where they often experienced harsh treatment and conditions.

In this total war, suffering extended far beyond battlefields, affecting civilians and home fronts in manifold ways. As military personnel perished, millions of their family members became widows and orphans, faced with emotional anguish and economic distress. The conscription of agricultural laborers, destruction of farmland, and imposition of naval blockades resulted in widespread food shortages, hunger, and, in some cases, mass starvation. Chronic shortages of fuel and clothing added to the misery. Living in horrific conditions, noncombatants contracted many of the same contagious diseases as their military counterparts. Chief among them was an aggressive strain of influenza that swept the war-torn world in 1918, resulting in fifty million deaths. In addition, roughly ten million people became displaced during the conflict, either by fighting within their own countries or after fleeing across international borders.

Some populations also became victims of involuntary displacement, along with other forms of state-sponsored violence. Among the most vicious contemporary assaults on civilians occurred in the Ottoman Empire, where state and military authorities undertook a systematic campaign to exterminate Armenian Christians and other ethnic groups. Through mass executions, intentional starvation, and forced deportations, they killed at least 660,000 Armenian, Assyrian, and Greek people (and perhaps twice that many). Governmental and military authorities also committed mass atrocities against Jewish

communities in imperial Russia, Serbian communities in the
Austro-Hungarian Empire, and other ethnic and religious
minorities, subjecting these populations to massacres, mass rape,
and acts of torture. All told, an estimated ten million civilians lost
their lives during the First World War. Tens of millions more
experienced its horrific effects in some way.

The Great War produced incalculable suffering, yet it also gave
rise to unparalleled efforts to *relieve* that suffering. Building on
the institutional and legal structures that were constructed from
the 1860s onward, humanitarian organizations and movements
experimented with diverse methods of aiding soldiers and
noncombatants, endeavoring to tame the horrors of total war.

Many humanitarians focused their attention on the battlefield,
striving to assist soldiers, sailors, and the medical personnel who
treated them. In theory, the Geneva and Hague Conventions had
been put in place to humanize and regulate warfare. Yet in
practice, militaries often made a mockery of international
humanitarian law. Much of the carnage and destruction that
states committed, moreover, was perfectly legal. The Geneva-based
ICRC, averring its neutrality and impartiality, spent the war
cataloging violations of the Geneva and Hague Conventions and
imploring belligerents to abide by their treaty obligations. In 1918,
the ICRC also launched appeals against the use of "asphyxiant and
poisonous gases," calling on states to ban chemical weapons and
rekindle their "feeling of humanity." Still a small organization with
limited resources, however, the ICRC struggled to extract any
significant reforms or concessions from the warring nations.

As stipulated by the Geneva Convention, responsibility for aiding
sick and wounded troops fell primarily to National Red Cross and
Red Crescent Societies. Although the ICRC exhorted these
voluntary associations to respect the principles of neutrality,
impartiality, and independence, it exerted no direct authority over
their operations. National Red Cross and Red Crescent Societies

served, above all, as medical auxiliaries to their own nations' militaries. During the war, volunteers joined and donated to their National Societies in droves, many of them motivated more by patriotism than by the principle of humanity. Even neutral countries saw a considerable bump in membership and funding, as wartime mobilization for humanitarian causes became a worldwide phenomenon.

Buoyed by this enthusiastic support, National Red Cross and Red Crescent Societies organized a dense web of humanitarian activities for soldiers and sailors. Their personnel administered field hospitals, ambulance units, hospital ships, sanitary trains, and medical clinics. Physicians and nurses bandaged wounds, performed surgeries, and treated illnesses and infections. In many countries, Red Cross and Red Crescent personnel also oversaw soldiers' convalescence and rehabilitation. Additionally, they organized recreational facilities for the mental health and morale of servicemen, such as canteens and rest houses. While these activities were most extensive in Europe, Red Cross and Red Crescent operations extended to many other places affected by the war, including North and East Africa, India, Japan, and the United States.

Assisting prisoners of war became another central activity for the International Red Cross and Red Crescent Movement. Though its efforts remained limited in most areas, the ICRC greatly expanded its remit in this particular humanitarian field. Its delegates began inspecting prisoner-of-war camps, assessing both their material conditions and the treatment of detainees. ICRC leaders discretely shared delegates' negative reports with offending governments, attempting to sway them toward more humane detention policies. Additionally, the ICRC established an International Prisoners-of-War Agency, which collected information about detainees to share with concerned family members. Three thousand people eventually volunteered or worked for the agency, making the exchange of messages between prisoners of war and their families a cornerstone of the ICRC's broadening mission. Many National Red Cross and Red Crescent Societies became involved with aiding prisoners of war, too. Most notably, they served as channels of communication and material aid, delivering mail, parcels, and relief supplies to detainees.

The ICRC and the National Red Cross and Red Crescent Societies played an outsized role in assisting military personnel, due to the recognition and protections afforded them by law and treaty, but they did not have a complete monopoly in this field. A host of NGOs provided complementary forms of assistance to soldiers. Voluntary associations like the Norton-Harjes Ambulance Corps, Society of Dutch Ambulances, and St. John Ambulance Brigade, for instance, played a crucial role in transporting wounded soldiers from battlefields to hospitals. Other groups operated far from the front lines. Some worked with disabled veterans, providing post-injury care and assisting in their rehabilitation. Improving troops' morale through the provision of gift packages, coffee, and recreational services became a core mission of many organizations, including Caritas, the South-West African Warriors' Association, and the Young Men's Christian Association. Still others concentrated on soldiers' families, raising funds to support their wives, children, and other dependents. Together, these voluntary efforts allowed for a more comprehensive approach to promoting soldiers' welfare and well-being.

Addressing the suffering of noncombatants, as opposed to soldiers, presented some distinct challenges. At the time, the Geneva Convention extended no formal protections to civilians, while the Hague Regulations contained only vague provisions, pertaining mainly to those living in occupied territories. Although the ICRC engaged in some advocacy efforts for civilians living in internment camps or under enemy occupation, it concentrated mainly on its founding mission—improving care for military personnel—throughout the duration of the war.

Compensating for the limited reach of the ICRC and international law, many other humanitarian organizations directed their energies to the home front, providing aid to children, women, refugees, and other noncombatants. A significant proportion of this voluntary aid flowed from the United States, a wealthy nation that remained relatively unscathed by the fighting. Among the earliest and most influential American humanitarian initiatives was the Commission for Relief in Belgium (CRB). Led by the mining engineer (and future president) Herbert Hoover, its personnel orchestrated the acquisition, importation, and distribution of foodstuffs for occupied Belgium and northern France, helping feed up to nine million people daily. Other leading organizations included the American Jewish Joint Distribution Committee, founded in 1914 to assist Jewish populations in central and eastern Europe, and the American Committee for Syrian and Armenian Relief, founded in 1915 to address civilian suffering within the Ottoman Empire.

After the United States entered the war in 1917, the American Red Cross became the nation's dominant relief agency. Fanning out across Allied Europe, Russia, and the Near East, American Red Cross personnel administered a far-reaching program of civilian relief. Operating in thousands of towns and cities, they cooperated with local populations to distribute food and clothing, administer hospitals and clinics, run schools and orphanages, and assist refugees in securing shelter and employment. They also undertook more ambitious projects, including public health campaigns against tuberculosis, fresh-air camps for children, and nursing schools for European women. By 1918, the American Red Cross had dwarfed its competition. Nevertheless, hundreds of other American relief organizations continued to send money, goods, and volunteers overseas. They targeted specific civilian populations and tackled an array of humanitarian problems. Together, these collective efforts fueled the United States' rise as a "humanitarian superpower," a position it maintained in decades to come.

Even as US aid efforts multiplied, citizens of other nations, both belligerent and neutral, extended their own forms of aid to noncombatants—including the millions who received little or no US assistance at all. Their aid flowed through hundreds of different channels, including National Red Cross and Red Crescent Societies, churches and voluntary organizations, patriotic funds and wartime charities, and agencies established by their governments. Like their American counterparts, most endeavored to address civilians' immediate needs for food, clothing, medical care, and resettlement. Some organizations took a more expansive approach, dealing with broader health, welfare, and sanitation problems among noncombatant populations. Though neglected by the laws of war, civilians became, thanks to these collective efforts, primary objects of international humanitarian concern.

Even so, noncombatants enjoyed no legal right to aid and few guarantees of protection. As aid organizations decided which populations to assist, feelings of national or cultural affinity routinely trumped the principles of neutrality and humanity. Within warring countries, humanitarian agencies tended to prioritize their own nationals and home fronts. Most international assistance, meanwhile, hewed closely to wartime alliances. Japanese relief organizations, for instance, sent considerable monetary and material aid to civilians in occupied Belgium. German missionaries and diplomats, likewise, established soup kitchens for starving civilians in Beirut, Tripoli, and other parts of the Ottoman Empire. Pushing against these currents, a few humanitarian organizations strove to deliver international aid on an impartial basis. The Friends' War Victims' Relief Committee, a British Quaker aid organization, adopted an official policy of nondiscrimination. Its personnel aided civilians in France, Germany, Russia, and elsewhere, purposefully ignoring battle lines. The Red Cross Societies of Argentina, Sweden, Switzerland, and other neutral nations also delivered aid to noncombatants on both sides of the conflict. Yet in most cases, political and military

5. During the First World War, humanitarian organizations like the French agency Le Secours de Guerre provided assistance to soldiers and civilians alike. Posters like this one helped to mobilize donations and public support.

alliances determined the reach of humanitarian aid. In total war, relief itself had become a weapon.

The Great War's hostilities officially ended with the signing of the Armistice of November 11, 1918. The humanitarian crisis it unleashed, however, was far from over. Fighting continued in some parts of the world, and widespread suffering persisted even as the guns fell silent. Nevertheless, the ceasefire and its promise of peace gave humanitarians a chance to reflect on their experiences during the war—and their plans for the future.

Between 1914 and 1918, people around the world employed a variety of practical and legal mechanisms to reduce the war's carnage. Their actions undoubtedly saved countless lives and helped alleviate physical and emotional distress among soldiers and civilians. Nevertheless, humanitarians were not immune to controversy or criticism. Their efforts often met with considerable pushback, stemming from governmental and military authorities, local charities and medical professionals, and relief recipients themselves. Critics accused humanitarians—often for good reason—of being overly controlling and paternalistic. They denounced humanitarian assistance for being driven by politics, ethnic and religious affinities, and personal ties, rather than by genuine need. These critics had a point. Heavily concentrated on the Western Front of Europe, international aid flowed less heavily into eastern Europe, Russia, and the Ottoman Empire, and only trickled into the war-torn colonies of Africa and Asia.

The conflict also revealed critical problems with the international humanitarian system in its current form. For all the legal and bureaucratic initiatives meant to soften war's horrors, battle had only grown deadlier and more brutal for combatants. Militaries routinely violated the laws of war. Aid workers encountered numerous obstacles to protecting civilians and displaced persons.

Divergent goals, poor coordination, and competition for resources led to infighting within the International Red Cross and Red Crescent Movement and among many nongovernmental aid organizations. Amid the Great War, conflicts raged over the purpose and character of humanitarianism itself. Resolving these issues became a priority for humanitarians in the decades that followed.

Chapter 4
From one world war to another

The Great War, the British writer H. G. Wells prophesied in 1914, was to be "the war that will end war." Had this prediction come to fruition, the work of many humanitarian organizations would have been rendered obsolete. Of course, idealistic visions of a world without conflict never materialized. Yet for people living through this tumultuous time, the official end of the war in 1919 prompted a reconsideration of humanitarianism's meaning and purpose in a postwar world.

Over the next several years, humanitarian organizations grappled with the human consequences and social upheaval that four-and-a-half years of fighting had wrought. At the same time, they undertook a variety of novel initiatives, centered on public health, disaster relief, child welfare, and other nonconflict concerns. Throughout the 1920s and into the 1930s, the international humanitarian system broadened its scope considerably, adapting to the challenges and possibilities of the new era.

Within a generation, any lingering hopes for a war-free world were shattered. Across the 1930s, inter- and intrastate violence erupted on multiple continents, eventually exploding into the Second World War. By the time that conflict concluded in 1945, it had precipitated an even greater humanitarian emergency than its predecessor, affecting hundreds of millions of people globally. Attempts to confront this mass suffering spurred fundamental changes in the international humanitarian system. Most notably, states and governments came to play a far more central and influential role in humanitarian affairs, assuming responsibilities that were once the domain of the voluntary sector.

As a new postwar era commenced in the late 1940s, humanitarianism continued to evolve. While responding to the devastation left in war's wake, governments and international organizations reformed the bureaucratic structures of modern humanitarianism and revised core tenets of international humanitarian law. Between 1919 and 1949, the international humanitarian system transformed, expanding to encompass new categories of suffering, new forms of humanitarian governance, and new strategies for mitigating the disasters of war and peace.

Rebuilding a war-torn world

For years after the First World War ended, the humanitarian crises it unleashed continued to reverberate. In the conflict's aftermath, problems of food scarcity, disease, and homelessness persisted throughout Europe, the Near East, and other theaters of war. Aggravating this already precarious situation, millions of demobilized soldiers, prisoners of war, and displaced civilians suddenly awaited repatriation, fueling a postwar refugee crisis across central and eastern Europe and Asia Minor. Hundreds of thousands of additional refugees fled the Russian Civil War, ongoing since the 1917 Bolshevik Revolution. The onset of famine in 1921 made conditions in Russia still worse. To the south, the Turkish War of Independence, which raged from 1919 to 1923, spawned armed violence on the battlefield and mass atrocities against ethnic and religious minorities. These issues represented only a fraction of the total human suffering in a world that was ostensibly at peace.

Responding to this grim situation, many humanitarian organizations remained in operation long after the 1918 armistice. As they had during the war, US-based organizations continued to play a significant role in postwar relief. The American Red Cross, for one, maintained hundreds of personnel abroad as late as June 1922. Concentrating their efforts in eastern Europe and Siberia, they distributed food and supplies among civilians and administered hundreds of health clinics, orphanages, schools, and workshops. Other American voluntary organizations, both faith-based and secular, made a similar shift from wartime to postwar aid. Reflecting this change in emphasis best was the American Committee for Syrian and Armenian Relief. In 1919, its leaders adopted a new name—Near East Relief—and an updated mission, assisting refugees and other civilians in the Eastern Mediterranean region. By 1921, Near East Relief operated dozens of orphanages across Turkey, Syria, Palestine, and the Caucasus region, which housed some 100,000 children.

In early 1919, the US government also established a brand-new aid agency, the American Relief Administration (ARA), greatly expanding the nation's—and the state's—humanitarian reach. Financed by a $100 million congressional appropriation and substantial private donations, the ARA's personnel oversaw the distribution of more than four million tons of food in twenty-one countries. This aid helped sustain some eighty million people by 1923. Controversially, this included citizens of the defeated Central Powers and victims of famine in Soviet Russia, perceived enemies of the United States. The decision to aid these populations was motivated less by the principles of neutrality and impartiality than it was by strategic political calculations. By tackling the problem of hunger and demonstrating American compassion, US officials aspired to save Europe from communism, or what they termed "the delirium of Bolshevism."

Although many war survivors welcomed this outpouring of American assistance, the sheer dominance of US aid organizations bred resentment in some corners. So did the arrogance and manifestly political aims that some American aid workers exhibited. Countering the United States' humanitarian largesse, people and governments in other countries pursued many alternate channels of assistance, charting their own postwar path.

The International Red Cross and Red Crescent Movement occupied a central role in these efforts, further consolidating its position as the world's most influential humanitarian network. The International Committee of the Red Cross (ICRC) devoted sustained attention to prisoners of war. Its delegates negotiated with governments to secure the release of detained soldiers and assisted with their subsequent repatriation. Going beyond its traditional remit, the ICRC also extended some assistance to noncombatants. Its delegates helped to feed starving civilians in defeated countries and to resettle Russian and Armenian refugees. Many National Red Cross and Red Crescent Societies organized postwar relief programs as well.

New humanitarian organizations also appeared on the scene, many of them committed to the principles of impartiality and international cooperation. An influential example was Save the Children, one of the first international nongovernmental organizations (INGOs) devoted to humanitarian causes. Founded in 1919 by British sisters Dorothy Buxton and Eglantyne Jebb, Save the Children's original mission was to nourish starving babies in defeated Central Powers nations. Buxton and Jebb soon split over their visions for the organization. Taking the helm, Jebb built Save the Children into an avowedly nonpolitical humanitarian association, designed to assist "innocent" youth "regardless of race, nationality, or creed." In 1920, Jebb went on to establish the Save the Children International Union. Headquartered in Geneva, it became an umbrella organization for child welfare organizations across Europe and the British Empire, and eventually much of the world.

While INGOs like the Save the Children linked humanitarian efforts across borders, so did a landmark intergovernmental organization (IGO), the League of Nations. Though the League is often remembered for its rather unsuccessful efforts to prevent war and resolve international disputes, it also made important contributions to postwar humanitarianism, serving as an effective forum for international collaboration in this area.

The League of Nations' entry into the humanitarian field began soon after its creation. In 1920, its leadership invited the Norwegian explorer and scientist Fridtjof Nansen to organize the repatriation of 430,000 prisoners held by Russia and the former Central Powers. The League then appointed Nansen to help resettle Russians displaced by civil war and famine. Over the next several years, Nansen's charge expanded to include Greek, Turkish, Armenian, and other refugees and stateless people. In 1922, Nansen also brokered a landmark interstate agreement that enabled stateless refugees to travel across borders with a League of Nations certificate. This "Nansen Passport," as it became known, was eventually issued to 450,000 asylum seekers.

Alongside these efforts to assist refugees, the League established specialized agencies devoted to international health, social welfare, and other nonconflict concerns. The League's early attention to these matters reflected a pair of broader shifts occurring within humanitarian circles. First, humanitarian organizations and movements were focusing more on peacetime problems, no longer prioritizing the consequences of armed conflict so heavily. Second, rather than just alleviating suffering after the fact, humanitarians were taking steps to *prevent* suffering from occurring by tackling its root causes.

Further steering these developments was another new international League: the League of Red Cross Societies (LRCS). This initiative was the brainchild of Henry Davison, the wartime head of the American Red Cross. Davison considered the ICRC's traditional focus on conflict to be too narrow. He conceived of organizing the world's National Red Cross Societies into a new peacetime federation, dedicated to improving public health, preventing disease, and responding to disasters. On May 5, 1919, Davison met with representatives of the British, French, Italian, and Japanese Red Cross Societies in Paris to establish the LRCS, making his vision a reality.

The response to this new Red Cross federation was decidedly mixed. At the Paris Peace Conference, US President Woodrow Wilson succeeded in securing an international endorsement for the LRCS, enshrined as Article 25 of the League of Nations Covenant. In Geneva, by contrast, the reception was far icier. The ICRC had not given its assent to Davison's actions. Incensed at his brash attempts to seize control of the International Red Cross and Red Crescent Movement, ICRC leadership initially refused to formally recognize the LRCS. Undeterred, Davison and his associates moved ahead with their plans. Within a year, thirty National Red Cross Societies joined the new federation and the LRCS officially commenced operations.

Over the next several years, the ICRC and LRCS sparred over their respective peacetime agendas. During the early 1920s, the LRCS made some preliminary strides toward coordinating Red Cross public health and disaster relief efforts. The ICRC, meanwhile, expanded into these very same fields. In 1920, it began administering a large endowment from the Japanese Red Cross called the Shôken Fund, using it to finance international disaster aid, anti-tuberculosis campaigns, nursing schools, and other peacetime projects.

Although leaders of the ICRC and LRCS took some tentative steps towards coexistence, it was not until 1928 that the two bodies achieved a meaningful rapprochement. Adopting shared statutes, they agreed to coexist as autonomous yet complementary bodies within the International Red Cross and Red Crescent Movement. As a general rule, the ICRC resumed its traditional mission of aiding victims of armed conflicts and serving as the guardian of international humanitarian law; disaster relief, public health, and other nonconflict issues became the LRCS's domain. Yet in practice, the lines between wartime and peacetime humanitarianism often blurred, confounding their respective missions, mandates, and fields of operation in the decades ahead.

Peacetime humanitarianism in the first postwar era

By the mid-1920s, the devastation the Great War created was finally subsiding. Over the next fifteen years, humanitarian organizations and movements grappled with a wide range of problems other than war. No longer concentrated in Europe and the Near East, these activities stretched into Africa, Asia, and the Americas, where they influenced both imperial and interstate relations.

A key humanitarian priority during the 1920s and 1930s was improving the international response to disasters. Across these decades, catastrophes like the 1923 Great Kantō Earthquake in Japan, the 1931 Central China floods, and the 1939 Chillán earthquake in Chile upended tens of millions of lives globally. In an effort to mitigate the suffering caused by natural hazards, humanitarians developed two distinct channels of international cooperation.

One of these avenues was through the League of Red Cross Societies. The LRCS Secretariat did not respond to disasters directly. Rather, it collected and shared information about catastrophes with National Red Cross and Red Crescent Societies, urging them to respond. As importantly, it helped to coordinate and facilitate those relief efforts. After conducting its first such appeal in 1922, the LRCS went on to organize disaster relief efforts for several dozen countries by the late 1930s. The LRCS also launched initiatives to study disasters and their prevention and to develop National Societies' response capabilities, becoming a recognized leader in this humanitarian field.

Alongside these nongovernmental efforts, a new organization called the International Relief Union orchestrated intergovernmental responses to disaster—or attempted to, at any rate. First proposed in 1921 by the head of the Italian Red Cross, plans for an intergovernmental disaster relief agency came to fruition with the active support of the League of Nations. In 1927, following several years of preparations, representatives from forty-three nations convened in Geneva to establish the International Relief Union. Its mandate was to administer an international relief fund, financed by contributions from member states, for use following sudden disasters of "exceptional gravity." Although beneficial in theory, the International Relief Union proved ineffectual in practice. Plagued from the start by financial and bureaucratic setbacks, it became active only in 1932; it then organized a handful of tepid disaster responses before essentially going defunct. Even so, its creation represented a historic step toward intergovernmental cooperation on peacetime humanitarian matters.

Under the auspices of the League of Nations, states also collaborated on many other international health and welfare activities. During the 1920s and 1930s, personnel of the League of Nations Health Organisation, led by the Polish physician and bacteriologist Ludwik Rajchman until 1938, developed the world's first comprehensive system of health, medicine, and sanitation. After an initial campaign against typhus in Russia and eastern Europe, the agency's international staff of experts organized commissions to tackle many other infectious diseases globally, including malaria, sleeping sickness, tuberculosis, and yellow fever. They developed new systems of epidemiological surveillance, collected health data and statistics, and devised international standards for drugs and vaccines. By the 1930s, the agency's mission expanded to include social and environmental problems, such as nutrition, housing, child welfare, and rural hygiene.

Complementing this work was the League's Social Questions and Opium Traffic Section. Headed by the British nurse and reformer Dame Rachel Crowdy until 1931, and then by Swedish diplomat Eric Ekstrand, this bureau housed committees and commissions devoted to multiple global concerns. It led campaigns to suppress the international traffic of women and girls for commercial sex. In cooperation with the International Labour Organization, its staff worked to abolish the slave trade in Ethiopia and the Arabian Peninsula. Additionally, they lobbied against coercive and compulsory labor regimes in colonial Africa, encouraging European empires to reform these abusive systems. Finally, the Social Section tried to stem the production, use, and international trafficking of opium and other narcotics. Though the characterization may sound odd to modern ears, Crowdy and her associates explicitly described these assorted projects as "humanitarian activities." Only by improving international social, health, and economic conditions, they insisted, could states hope to preserve world peace.

Many nongovernmental organizations (NGOs) also focused on social issues, which often blurred the lines between humanitarian relief and development assistance. Illustrating this evolving emphasis, once again, was the American organization Near East Relief. During the 1920s, moving away from its postwar efforts to feed and house refugees, the organization devoted increasing resources toward long-term development projects. These included vocational schools, rural health campaigns, agricultural demonstrations, and other technical assistance programs. Less concerned with saving individual lives, its personnel now aspired to reform the territories of the former Ottoman Empire, seeking to modernize these societies along Western lines. In 1930, leadership once again renamed the organization to reflect its updated mission, rebranding it the Near East Foundation.

Child welfare represented another leading cause for many voluntary humanitarian organizations. In early 1923, hoping to inspire more action on this issue, the International Save the Children Union proclaimed the Declaration of the Rights of the Child. According to its tenets, all children possessed universal rights to a "normal development," including basic care and nurturing, protection from exploitation, and "relief in times of distress." Adopted by the League of Nations the following year, the Geneva Declaration (as it became known) reflected a burgeoning emphasis on youth within both humanitarian and political circles.

Save the Children went on to organize a Conference on the African Child in 1931, attempting to showcase its commitment to universality. Held in Geneva, the conference brought two hundred European missionaries, reformers, and politicians together with a small handful of African delegates. For several days, they discussed strategies to improve the health and well-being of African youth. The composition of attendees was hardly equitable, and the conference resulted in few material improvements. Yet in its time, it signaled a budding concern with cross-continental humanitarian issues and an effort to pursue more meaningful forms of international cooperation.

In addition to conducting activities for children, some organizations promoted humanitarianism *by* young people. The Junior Red Cross Movement was an especially influential vehicle for these efforts. In 1922, building on earlier initiatives at the national level, the League of Red Cross Societies established an international Junior Red Cross program, designed to mobilize youth for humanitarian purposes. With the League's energetic promotion, Junior Red Cross Societies spread rapidly around the world. By the 1930s, branches existed in multiple European and Latin American nations, Canada and the United States, Japan,

India and South Africa, and several other countries and colonies. Counting tens of millions of young members, the Junior Red Cross constituted a major international humanitarian movement in its own right.

Junior Red Cross activities originally centered on aiding children in war-torn Europe, but the mission steadily shifted toward the promotion of child welfare and international education. Throughout the 1920s and 1930s, Junior Red Cross activities taught children basic principles of health and hygiene. They encouraged young people to participate in service activities within their own communities and for people overseas. Through its international correspondence program, the Junior Red Cross facilitated exchanges of letters, drawings, and handmade gifts between children in different nations. It also provided pedagogical

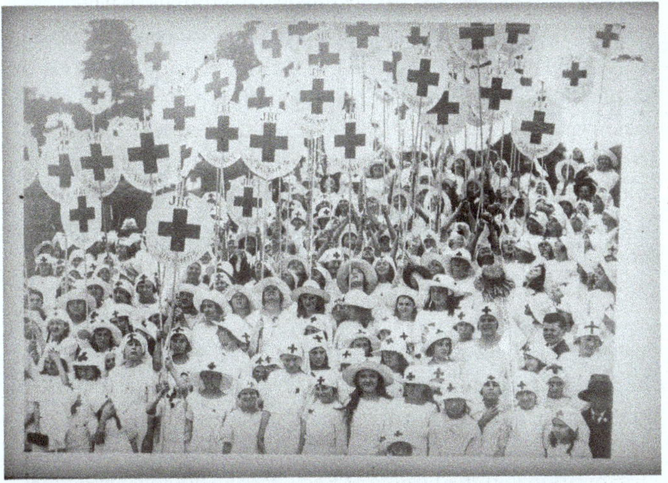

6. **Humanitarianism by and for young people became a global phenomenon between the two world wars. Organizations like the Junior Red Cross mobilized millions of youth members, including the five thousand school children who attended this pageant in Sydney, Australia.**

materials to teachers, designed to promote "education for world understanding." Collectively, these activities contributed to humanitarianism's ever-broadening definition in the postwar era.

For all the good humanitarians achieved—or aspired to achieve—through their peacetime programs, their attempts to remake the postwar world had some notable limitations. First, humanitarianism remained a key justification for empire. As calls for independence mounted across Africa, South Asia, and the Caribbean during the 1920s and 1930s, in fact, defenders of colonialism doubled down on this age-old claim. Hoping to placate critics and prove their legitimacy, imperial governments spearheaded a host of colonial development projects. Officials defined these initiatives in patently humanitarian terms, pledging to lift colonized people out of poverty, modernize their societies, and improve their lives. In reality, these schemes failed to materially transform the deeply unequal conditions in which colonized peoples lived and labored. In many cases, humanitarian rhetoric served as little more than a fig leaf, disguising the realities of colonial violence, racism, and exploitation. Although organizations like Save the Children and the League of Nations Health and Social Sections tried to reform the worst abuses of colonial rule, moreover, most of their personnel had no intention of dismantling the imperial system. They sought to make empires more ethical, more productive, and more cooperative, not to radically upend the status quo.

Second, despite the professed emphasis on transborder cooperation, the international humanitarian system remained heavily dominated by European and North American interests. Compared with predecessors, organizations like the League of Nations Health Organisation and the League of Red Cross Societies succeeded in including a greater range of voices, particularly from Latin America and East Asia. Even so, US and western European experts, organizations, and governments exerted disproportionate influence over humanitarian decision-making. These power dynamics were even more potent in the field. European and American aid workers often behaved paternalistically, even arrogantly, toward populations they assisted. They also repeatedly interfered in less powerful nations in the name of rescuing women, abolishing slavery, combatting opium, and other causes, perpetuating the fraught tradition of humanitarian intervention.

Facing external pressures and foreign meddling, many communities strove to maintain indigenous humanitarian traditions and practices. When drought and famine struck northern China in the early 1920s, for instance, Chinese social networks, military authorities, and households together mobilized assistance for millions of migrants and other destitute people, acting well before any international aid arrived. After a major earthquake destroyed Managua—then under US military occupation—in 1931, many Nicaraguans rejected the relief offered by US Marines, relying instead on assistance from El Salvador, Mexico, and other neighboring countries. Comparable instances of local and regional solidarity arose across many corners of the postwar world. Yet as humanitarianism grew more enmeshed with interstate relations and imperial governance during the 1920s and 1930s, indigenous and international efforts routinely collided and clashed. Although many communities strove to maintain their traditional humanitarian customs and values, the boundaries between local and global humanitarianisms steadily continued to erode.

Once more unto the breach

Even as they undertook a panoply of peacetime activities during the 1920s and 1930s, humanitarian organizations and movements never fully ignored armed conflict. Memories of the Great War remained vivid and haunting. Alongside idealistic hopes for peace, fears of renewed conflict lingered. As those fears came to fruition, the international humanitarian system prepared for—and ultimately responded to—the horrors of another world war.

One early postwar priority was to revise international humanitarian law. During the 1920s, the ICRC drafted a supplement to the existing Geneva Conventions, intended to establish new protections for detained soldiers and sailors. In 1929, the Swiss government convened a diplomatic conference in Geneva to approve the new treaty. Signed by forty-six nations, the Geneva Convention relative to the Treatment of Prisoners of War entered into force two years later. Among its other provisions, the Geneva Convention of 1929 established principles governing the humane treatment of detained troops. It also required states to collect and share information about detainees and formalized the ICRC's authority to inspect prisoner-of-war camps.

While the 1929 Geneva Convention—the first revision since 1906—established new legal safeguards for imprisoned troops, calls to extend similar protections to noncombatants made little headway. Another twenty years were to pass before civilians were incorporated into this pillar of international humanitarian law.

After a relative and welcome lull during the 1920s, warfare resurfaced as a focal point of international humanitarian concern during the early 1930s, with the Japanese invasion of Manchuria in 1931 and the outbreak of the Chaco War between Paraguay and Bolivia in 1932. Conflicts continued to erupt across the remainder of the decade, including the Italo-Ethiopian War in 1935, the Spanish Civil War in 1936, and the Second Sino-Japanese War in 1937, sparked by Japan's full-scale invasion of China. All the while, internal violence flared in several countries, including most notably Nazi Germany and the Stalinist Soviet Union. In late 1939, most European powers descended into war, dragging their colonial empires in with them. The Second World War had commenced.

The road to war in the 1930s was paved with humanitarian crises. Across the various theaters of conflict, professional soldiers, armed rebels, and volunteer forces engaged in bloody combat, often showing complete disregard for the Geneva and Hague Conventions. Reports of chemical warfare, aerial bombing of cities, extrajudicial killings, mass rape, and other atrocities mounted. Around the world, millions of people became displaced due to fighting, upheaval, and persecution. And this was all *before* 1939, when the Second World War rapidly intensified.

Though there were some valiant attempts to address this widespread suffering, on the whole the international humanitarian system proved either unequipped or unwilling to confront the spiraling crises of the 1930s. Many states resisted becoming involved in humanitarian issues. Already grappling with the global Great Depression, most government leaders feared being dragged into war or inviting problems into their own countries. As a result, relatively little state-sponsored humanitarian aid flowed into Ethiopia, Spain, China, and other war zones. Governments also overwhelmingly refused to receive Jewish refugees who attempted to flee Nazi persecution, preventing millions from escaping the coming horrors of the Holocaust. Though voluntary organizations contributed some aid to the warring nations, their efforts proved woefully insufficient, incapable of ameliorating the soaring distress among soldiers and civilians.

Reasserting its moral and legal authority in wartime humanitarian matters, the ICRC intervened in multiple conflicts during the 1930s as a neutral intermediary. It sent delegations to China, Bolivia and Paraguay, Ethiopia, and Spain, charged with visiting prisoner-of-war camps and reminding belligerents to respect the international laws of war. These efforts to humanize warfare, however, met with only marginal success. Several states refused to allow ICRC representatives to access their detention camps. Lacking enforcement mechanisms, delegates stood by as militaries flagrantly violated the laws of war and attacked civilian targets. Amid these setbacks, the ICRC did catalog a few achievements. In 1935, Emperor Haile Selassie agreed to organize the Ethiopian Red Cross, the first noncolonial African National Red Cross

Society. During the Spanish Civil War, ICRC delegates administered food relief efforts for civilian populations and assisted refugees in France, acting outside the scope of the Geneva Convention to aid these noncombatants. Yet, overall, limited resources and uncooperative belligerents constrained the ICRC's actions in the field.

Horrific as they were, the more localized humanitarian crises of the 1930s were only the prelude to a far greater global catastrophe. Beginning in 1939, the Second World War escalated rapidly, eventually affecting just about every corner of the globe. Like the Great War before it—but on an even vaster scale—this conflict gave rise to a tremendous humanitarian emergency. By the time hostilities officially ceased in 1945, an estimated seventy-five million people had died worldwide. The majority of them were civilians. Armed violence on the battlefield, systematic murders and mass atrocities, urban bombing campaigns, and deplorable conditions in forced labor and concentration camps all contributed to this staggering death toll. The impacts on survivors were no less ghastly, with untold numbers suffering from physical injuries, psychological wounds, hunger, and serious illnesses. As many as sixty-five million people in Europe and a hundred million in China became either internally or externally displaced because of conflict. Elsewhere in the world, tens of millions of additional refugees were forced from their homes.

This collective devastation presented the international humanitarian system with its greatest challenge to date. The response, in turn, was without historical parallel. Between 1939 and 1945, governments, international organizations, and voluntary relief associations mobilized a comprehensive and far-reaching set of relief and rehabilitation activities. In the process, they transformed international humanitarianism itself.

The International Red Cross and Red Crescent Movement played a prominent role in these efforts, performing a wider range of humanitarian activities than in any previous conflict. As in earlier wars, ICRC delegates inspected camps for prisoners of war and civilian detainees, making eleven thousand such visits by war's end. Staff of the ICRC's Central Agency for Prisoners of War also collected information on detained soldiers and shared it with their families. Additionally, they oversaw the exchange of 120 million letters between prisoners and their loved ones. Alongside these more traditional activities for military personnel, efforts for civilians multiplied. Coming together in neutral Geneva, the ICRC and the LRCS established a Joint Relief Commission to facilitate cooperation on behalf of all war victims. Under its auspices, the two bodies orchestrated the delivery and distribution of 165,000 tons of food, medicines, and other critical supplies, aiding children, women, refugees, and other noncombatants in multiple war-torn countries.

While the ICRC and LRCS worked to expand their own spheres of influence, they found themselves operating in an increasingly crowded humanitarian field. On every continent, nongovernmental organizations and movements competed to raise funds, collect supplies, and recruit volunteers. Many of the groups founded during these years proved temporary, but some—including the International Rescue Committee, the Oxford Committee for Famine Relief (Oxfam), and Catholic Relief Services—were to remain influential players in the international humanitarian system for decades to come. Within warring and neutral nations alike, large swaths of the population became involved in these organizations and movements, propelling grass-roots humanitarianism into a global cultural phenomenon.

Although many nations saw an explosion of voluntary relief initiatives during the 1940s, the wealth and influence of the United States' aid sector remained unmatched. As they had during the First World War, American Catholic, Jewish, Protestant, and secular organizations administered a dense web of overseas relief activities. Yet in a striking contrast to that earlier conflict, the US government now operated right alongside them, significantly

7. **During and after the Second World War, humanitarian organizations provided vast amounts of aid to soldiers, prisoners of war, and noncombatants. Aid came from governments, voluntary agencies, and both existing and new international organizations. Here, formerly imprisoned French soldiers receive supplies and sustenance after being liberated.**

expanding its role in humanitarian affairs. Through the President's War Relief Control Board, established in 1942, federal officials assumed broad powers to regulate and manage the foreign aid efforts of American voluntary organizations. More directly, government officials began delivering food, medical assistance, and other humanitarian relief through state and military channels, including the Lend-Lease Program and the Office of Foreign Relief and Rehabilitation Operations. Grasping the diplomatic and strategic importance of humanitarian assistance to the broader war effort, US government officials brought foreign aid under the state's purview.

Such developments were hardly unique to the United States. Throughout the war, other national governments extended similar controls over their countries' private aid sectors. Around the globe, state agencies, colonial offices, and militaries performed a wide range of humanitarian activities, from organizing food and clothing distributions to administering health clinics and refugee camps. Together, these trends reflected a pair of broad, intertwined patterns sweeping the war-torn world. Humanitarianism was becoming more central to foreign policy planning and wartime strategy; this led states, in turn, to assume a more active role in humanitarian governance.

In a further indication of this shift, governments began pursuing new multilateral channels of humanitarian cooperation. The most significant of these international initiatives was the United Nations Relief and Rehabilitation Administration (UNRRA). Founded in November 1943 by forty-four Allied governments, UNRRA focused initially on providing emergency relief to populations living under Allied control. Its large staff—numbering more than ten thousand—provided food, clothing, shelter, and basic medical care to civilians throughout central and eastern Europe, including in the liberated territories of Italy, Austria, and Germany. UNRAA also established smaller missions in China, Korea, and the Philippines. UNRAA relied heavily on US funding for its operations, with the US government contributing roughly 70 percent of its total expenditures. Even so, the agency represented a bold new experiment in interstate relief, part of the wider trend toward increased governmental involvement in humanitarian issues.

By 1945, the international humanitarian system had taken unparalleled steps to aid the victims of total war, changing considerably in the process. Concurrent with these achievements, however, were some grievous failures to protect certain populations and to confront particular forms of suffering.

Among the most infamous was the abject failure to protect European Jews and other victims of the Holocaust. Throughout

8. **The United Nations Relief and Rehabilitation Administration (UNRRA) marked an important step toward intergovernmental cooperation on humanitarian issues. During the Second World War and its aftermath, its personnel administered a broad slate of emergency relief and longer-term recovery assistance projects around the world, including the provision of fresh fish to this refugee reception center in Shanghai, China.**

the war, the Nazi government refused to permit ICRC visits to concentration camps in German territories. Details of the persecution and systematic murder of Jewish populations nevertheless leaked, reaching Geneva as early as 1942. For the next three years, the ICRC's leadership chose neither to denounce these atrocities publicly nor even to exert quiet pressure on Nazi officials. In the face of genocide, they prioritized the principle of neutrality over the principled commitment to humanity. Sixty years later, the institution's leadership declared this inaction on the Holocaust "the greatest failure in the history of the ICRC."

Another notable limitation was the vastly unequal distribution of humanitarian aid. Despite appalling suffering in China, the Middle East, North Africa, and elsewhere, the major players in the international humanitarian system directed the bulk of their resources toward Europe. UNRRA, for instance, delivered five times more aid to European countries than to all other parts of the world combined. ICRC and LRCS delegates, likewise, concentrated their operations on the European continent, undertaking only limited activities in East Asia and other theaters of war. Although Red Cross Societies expanded across sub-Saharan Africa during the 1940s, most (with the exception of the Ethiopian Red Cross) focused on assisting white European colonists rather than Black majority populations. Despite the United States' position as a "humanitarian superpower," the US government and American voluntary sector directed assistance mainly to Allied governments, leaving many war-torn countries untouched by American aid.

In the absence of substantial external assistance, populations outside of Europe turned once again to their own channels of humanitarian aid. In Sichuan Province, the center of Free China throughout the Japanese occupation, Chinese physicians provided extensive medical relief to soldiers and civilians. Privileging a hybrid approach to aid, they blended traditional Chinese medicine with Western medical practices. In North Africa, the colonies of Algeria, Morocco, and Tunisia all fell under the control of Fascist regimes during the early 1940s. Throughout these territories, Muslim leaders and community members sheltered many Jewish residents from Nazi and Vichy French authorities, a moving example of interfaith humanitarian action amid the Holocaust. When a severe famine gripped Bengal in 1943, the British colonial government's response proved wholly inadequate. Filling the humanitarian void left by the state, voluntary associations and private charities across India, together with Indian expatriates as far away as East Africa, contributed large amounts of food, money, and other relief. Their efforts helped sustain millions of starving Bengalis, preventing an already dire catastrophe from becoming still worse.

Although local and regional humanitarian networks like these provided crucial assistance during the Second World War, their efforts also laid bare one of the critical shortcomings of the international humanitarian system: its reach was not truly global. Coming to terms with this issue was just one of the myriad challenges facing humanitarians as a new postwar era dawned.

A new postwar era

On September 2, 1945, the Japanese government's surrender ended the Second World War's hostilities. But in the conflict's wake, a monumental humanitarian crisis remained. Across every theater of war, cities, towns, and villages lay in utter ruin. Millions of imprisoned soldiers awaited release and repatriation—even though many no longer had a home or even a country to return to. In Asia and Europe, tens of millions of new refugees joined the masses who were already displaced. A diverse lot, they included survivors of forced labor and concentration camps, uprooted ethnic minority populations, newly stateless people, and German and Japanese civilians expelled from former imperial outposts. Amplifying this already immense refugee crisis, the 1947 Partition of India and Pakistan, the establishment of the State of Israel and Palestinian expulsion in 1948, and the Chinese Civil War and 1949 Communist Revolution together triggered the flight or forced exodus of millions of additional people globally.

To confront these interlaced problems, many humanitarian organizations maintained active programs of postwar relief and recovery. The intergovernmental UNRRA, for one, continued to operate until 1947. Shifting away from emergency relief, UNRRA's postwar projects were geared toward the rehabilitation of Europe's agricultural and industrial sectors. Their aim was to restore the self-sufficiency of war survivors by boosting the productivity of farms and factories. In addition, UNRRA assumed the primary responsibility for repatriating millions of refugees and displaced persons. Its staff administered hundreds of resettlement camps across Europe and worked to coordinate refugees' return to their countries of origin. More than a million people refused repatriation, however, especially to the Soviet Union and its satellites. Their collective resistance fueled mounting debates over the rights of refugees to seek and declare asylum.

The ICRC and LRCS also became involved in a wide range of humanitarian crises. Acting on its principled commitment to impartiality and neutrality, the ICRC initially prioritized assistance for German civilians and prisoners of war. Already facing international criticism for its failure to condemn Nazi war crimes, the ICRC provoked the ire of many governments with this decision. Though weakened by these controversies, the ICRC and LRCS forged ahead with other activities, expanding their sights well beyond Europe. Following the Partition of India and Pakistan in 1947, the two organizations administered assistance efforts for refugees and prisoners in the Kashmir borderland. In 1948, they organized an even larger humanitarian operation for victims of the Arab-Israeli War, aiding both Jewish populations and newly displaced Palestinian refugees. During these same years, the LCRS returned to its traditional work of coordinating responses to disasters and promoting the development of National Red Cross and Red Crescent Societies, gradually resuming its foundational peacetime mission.

Joining these established organizations in the field were new specialized agencies of the United Nations (UN). Founded in 1945 to replace the League of Nations, the UN assumed a central role in postwar humanitarian governance. Multiple UN agencies focused on the protection of displaced and stateless people. They included the International Refugee Organization, which temporarily succeeded UNRRA, and its permanent successor, the Office of the UN High Commissioner for Refugees (UNHCR), founded in 1950. Additionally, the UN established the Relief and Works Agency for Palestinian Refugees (UNRWA) in 1949, charged with assisting the roughly 700,000 Palestinians displaced within and outside

Israel. Complementing the work of these agencies, the UN also led the development of an international agreement to protect refugees and their rights, ultimately codified in the 1951 Refugee Convention.

Other UN agencies, meanwhile, concentrated on a broad array of humanitarian issues, stemming from both conflict and peace. The UN Food and Agriculture Organization (FAO), founded in 1945, initially focused on addressing urgent postwar food shortages. However, it quickly went on to launch global initiatives related to hunger, nutrition, and agricultural development. Likewise, the UN International Children's Emergency Fund (UNICEF) was established in 1946 to aid children in war-torn Europe and China, but it soon adopted a much broader institutional mandate: to improve child and maternal welfare globally. The World Health Organization (WHO), founded in 1948, worked with member countries to control and prevent infectious diseases, improve public health and sanitation, and enhance their national medical services. Founded in the Second World War's wake, each of these agencies became crucial fixtures of nonconflict humanitarianism in the years ahead.

Arising in tandem with these efforts to relieve and rebuild the postwar world were movements to revise international humanitarian law. Since the early 1930s, global conflicts and state-sponsored violence had exposed glaring deficiencies in the Geneva and Hague Conventions. Most notably, they did little to protect noncombatants or victims of civil wars and other internal conflicts. In the late 1940s, now grappling with the realities of the Holocaust, the Nanjing Massacre, and other recent atrocities, states negotiated several landmark international accords intended to prevent similar horrors in the future. One key agreement came in 1948, when the United Nations adopted the Convention on the Prevention and Punishment of the Crime of Genocide. Blurring the lines between humanitarian law and another emerging field—international human rights law—the UN Genocide

Convention made the willful destruction of any "national, ethnical, racial or religious group" an international crime.

The following year, the signing of the 1949 Geneva Conventions marked a watershed in international humanitarian law. In April 1949, after years of planning, ICRC representatives and delegates from sixty-four nations assembled in Geneva to negotiate a sweeping overhaul of the laws of war. Five months later, the conference produced four distinct treaties. The First, Second, and Third Geneva Conventions replaced the existing Geneva treaties, updating and expanding the protections afforded to wounded and sick soldiers, sailors, and prisoners of war. The Fourth Geneva Convention represented the most dramatic update. For the first time, it extended comprehensive international protections to civilian populations during conflicts, including internees and those living in occupied territory. Another notable outcome of the conference was the adoption of Common Article 3. Applying to all four Geneva Conventions, it extended their rules and principles to civil wars and some other non-international armed conflicts.

The 1949 Geneva Conventions marked an ambitious and historic attempt to humanize warfare. And yet, even as states agreed to recognize new categories of suffering under the laws of war, they ignored or intentionally excluded many others. In Geneva, calls to regulate such matters as anticolonial rebellions, aerial and nuclear bombing, food blockades, and the rights of political prisoners made little headway. These and other issues were quashed by powerful governments, which sought to preserve maximum flexibility in warmaking and in domestic and imperial governance and policing. In the process of defining who counted as a "victim" of war, deserving of international protection, the Geneva Conventions' drafters demarcated the legal boundaries of humanity itself.

International humanitarian activities thus flourished across the late 1940s, as states and organizations collaborated to rebuild the shattered world. Yet during these same years, one nation remained a dominant force: the United States. As the world's wealthiest and most powerful country, the United States continued to exert a profound influence on postwar humanitarianism—and, by extension, on postwar international affairs.

A new and particularly influential American aid program in these years was the Cooperative for American Remittances to Europe, or CARE. Founded in late 1945 by twenty-two American voluntary organizations, CARE's original mission was to combat hunger in postwar Europe. To achieve this goal, the consortium coordinated the purchase and delivery of millions of food packages from individual US citizens to European civilians, promoting a novel form of person-to-person humanitarianism. Complementing this work, organizations like Catholic Relief Services, Church World Service, and Lutheran World Relief delivered considerable quantities of food, clothing, money, and other material relief to many war-torn countries. American voluntary organizations, it bears noting, did not act independently. They continued to cooperate closely with the US Departments of State and Agriculture to plan and deliver humanitarian assistance abroad, maintaining channels of state-private collaboration established during the war years.

Even greater amounts of aid flowed directly through US governmental channels, further intensifying the pattern of expanding state involvement in the humanitarian sphere. The most ambitious of these initiatives was the European Recovery Program, popularly known as the Marshall Plan. Established in 1948 by the US Congress, this program ultimately funneled more than $13 billion in assistance to sixteen European countries. With this aid, US policymakers sought to spur agricultural and industrial recovery within recipient nations. Guided more by political motivations than by genuine humanitarian sentiments, US officials aimed to prevent the spread of communism by nurturing free-market economies and stable democratic governments. In the late 1940s, aid was becoming a critical weapon in a nascent Cold War, a trend that hardened in the years ahead.

The United States may have dominated the humanitarian scene in the late 1940s, but it never possessed a complete monopoly on bilateral aid. As other nations recovered from the Second World War, moreover, many of them began to follow a similar path as the US government. In the decades ahead, states assumed increasing responsibility for the funding, coordination, and administration of humanitarian assistance, embracing foreign aid as a tool of their own foreign policy. Yet as governments, international organizations, and voluntary associations jockeyed for influence in an increasingly crowded field, long-standing debates over the principles, purposes, and best practices of global humanitarian governance only continued to multiply.

Chapter 5
Cold wars, hot wars, decolonization, and development

Reforged in the crucible of the two world wars and their aftermaths, the organizational and legal structures of modern humanitarianism changed considerably during the forty years that followed. Between the late 1940s and the late 1980s, a pair of overlapping geopolitical currents shaped humanitarianism's evolving trajectory.

One of them was the global Cold War. Though it is often described as an ideological rivalry between the United States and the Soviet Union, the Cold War is better understood as a worldwide contest, waged over competing visions of political and economic organization. Not limited to Europe and North America, debates over the merits of capitalist versus socialist systems rippled across Asia, Africa, Latin America, and the Middle East. In many places, these disagreements intersected with local tensions, giving rise to armed conflicts. Powerful states interfered repeatedly in these regional struggles, transforming them into proxy wars and greatly exacerbating their violence. For large swaths of the world's population, the Cold War was anything but cold.

The second key development was the process of decolonization and postcolonial state-building. In the decades after the Second World War, an increasing number of colonized societies cast off imperial rule to become independent nation-states. Some won independence through relatively peaceful means, others through bloody wars of national liberation. Either way, the results were revolutionary. Between 1945 and the mid-1960s, dozens of new nation-states emerged across the decolonizing world; by 1989, more than eighty new countries had come into existence worldwide. Formal independence, however, guaranteed neither peace nor prosperity. Many postcolonial states struggled to achieve political, economic, and social stability, leading to ongoing challenges and conflict.

In the throes of the global Cold War and decolonization, the international humanitarian system underwent several pivotal changes. First, as they responded to the suffering produced by colonial revolutions, postcolonial conflicts, and proxy wars, humanitarian organizations and movements became far more global in their reach. Navigating this complex and contested geopolitical terrain, however, led many organizations to revise their institutional missions and rethink their core principles. Second, humanitarians devoted increasing attention to the problems of international development. In postcolonial nations and other less wealthy countries, they administered both short-term relief and long-term projects to improve health and well-being, further blurring the boundaries between these categories of aid.

Finally, the humanitarian field grew more diverse—and more crowded—than ever before. The birth of dozens of new nation-states dramatically altered the composition of the international humanitarian system. As more and more formerly colonized peoples joined the United Nations, the International Red Cross and Red Crescent Movement, and other key institutions, they exercised greater sway over global humanitarian governance. The explosive growth of international governmental and nongovernment organizations also affected these dynamics, bringing a chorus of new voices into humanitarian decision-making. Together, these transformative shifts laid the bedrock for the contemporary humanitarian system.

From Europe to everywhere

For several years after the Second World War ended, Europe remained the primary locus of international humanitarian concern. As European societies recovered from the war, however, the flow of international aid steadily changed course. Starting in the late 1940s, humanitarian organizations and movements turned their attention elsewhere: to South and Southeast Asia, the Middle East, sub-Saharan and North Africa, and Central and South America.

As aid agencies moved into new fields during the 1950s and early 1960s, they also waded into the battlefields of the global Cold War. In this complex political milieu, humanitarian aid became a potent weapon, wielded by powerful states on both sides of the bipolar system. Eager to win hearts and minds and to promote the virtues of capitalism, the US government contributed rising amounts of food, money, and other assistance to postcolonial nations and other developing countries. So did Great Britain, France, West Germany, and other western European governments, which became leading donors of bilateral and multilateral aid. These Western governments collaborated closely with major voluntary organizations—including Save the Children, Oxfam, CARE, Caritas, Church World Service, and World Vision International—ensuring that private aid served state foreign policy objectives.

Their Communist rivals did much the same thing, fueling a global alms race. From the 1950s on, the Soviet Union and the Eastern Bloc countries established active programs of humanitarian relief and other forms of international assistance. After their respective revolutions in 1949 and 1959, China and Cuba followed suit. Through their foreign aid programs, these states sought to advertise the benefits of socialism while demonstrating solidarity with anti-imperial revolutions and postcolonial governments.

These patterns became visible as early as the Korean War. After the Second World War, US and Soviet military leaders divided Korea, a former Japanese colony, into two halves. Tensions immediately flared between the Soviet-backed Communist government in the North and the US-backed authoritarian government in the South. In June 1950, they escalated into armed violence. Though it originated as a civil conflict over Korea's political future, the Korean War became an iconic proxy war, fueled by superpower patrons and their allies.

The humanitarian response to this conflict adhered closely to Cold War battle lines. Averring its neutrality, the ICRC offered its services to both Korean governments. North Korean officials, however, repeatedly rebuffed these offers. Skeptical of the ICRC's professed impartiality, they denied delegates access to prisoners of war and civilian detention camps. As a result, the ICRC's humanitarian activities remained confined to the South.

Yet the bulk of South Korean relief and rehabilitation assistance did not come from the ICRC; it came from the country's allies. South Korean soldiers and civilians received abundant aid from the US government and military, American voluntary organizations, and two main UN agencies, the Civil Assistance Command for Korea and the Korean Reconstruction Agency. In addition to providing food, clothing, and medical care, US and UN personnel administered extensive agricultural and industrial recovery programs, designed to spur South Korean development along capitalist lines.

North of the 38th parallel, funds and supplies poured in from the Soviet Union, China, East Germany, Czechoslovakia, Hungary, and Poland. During the conflict, socialist countries organized solidarity rallies, coordinated fundraising appeals, and took in hundreds of North Korean orphans and students as refugees. After hostilities ceased in 1953, they sent experts in urban planning and heavy industry to North Korea to guide recovery and development. Humanitarian aid, not just military assistance, fueled the proxy war in Korea.

As the 1950s and 1960s progressed, Cold War dynamics shaped humanitarian activities in other conflicts, much as they had on the Korean Peninsula. Just as critical, however, were the forces of decolonization. As anticolonial struggles accelerated during these years, both empires and insurgencies weaponized and politicized humanitarianism, trying to harness it to their advantage.

National liberation wars in Africa provide a vivid example of the vexed links between humanitarianism and decolonization. In 1952, anticolonial rebels known as the Mau Mau launched an armed uprising against British colonial rule in Kenya. Two years later, the National Liberation Front in Algeria initiated a revolution of its own, fighting for independence from the French Empire. Both the Mau Mau uprising and Algerian Revolution devolved into extraordinarily violent conflicts. As Kenyan and Algerian guerilla forces took up armed resistance against colonial rule, British and French authorities responded with unchecked brutality. They subjected captured and suspected rebels to systematic torture, starvation, and summary executions. They forcibly uprooted Kenyan and Algerian civilians and confined them to internment camps, where disease and hunger ran rampant. In both conflicts, European-based voluntary organizations collaborated closely with colonial authorities, favoring French and British troops over the impartial delivery of aid. Algerians ultimately gained independence in 1962 and Kenyans in 1963, but only after sustained bloodshed and misery.

The conduct of these colonial wars sparked contentious debates over the reach of international humanitarian law and whose interests it was supposed to serve. As violence in Kenya and Algeria first started to intensify, the ICRC attempted to intervene as a neutral intermediary. In theory, Common Article 3 of the

1949 Geneva Conventions had extended the laws of war to internal conflicts, authorizing the ICRC's involvement. British and French officials, however, rejected this notion. They branded anticolonial forces as terrorists and criminals, not combatants. The situations in their colonies were "emergencies" and "civil disturbances," they insisted, not armed conflicts. As such, they fell outside the purview of international humanitarian law. Pushing back against these claims, the ICRC eventually gained limited access to detention camps in Algeria and Kenya. Faced with ongoing British and French resistance, however, its delegates struggled to ensure even minimum humanitarian standards.

Taking matters into their own hands—and tactically showcasing their own respect for the laws of war—Algerian nationalists advanced alternative interpretations of the Geneva Conventions. They demanded protections for anticolonial forces and Algerian war victims, and they publicly denounced the French military for its human rights abuses. Establishing an alternative to the French Red Cross, they also founded an Algerian Red Crescent Society in 1957. It monitored prisoners' conditions, raised funds and international awareness, and provided medical care and other aid to Algerian refugees. Despite these efforts, the ICRC did not recognize the Algerian Red Crescent as a legitimate National Society until 1963, the year after Algerian independence.

Along with the wars in Kenya and Algeria, the Congo Crisis of the early 1960s revealed humanitarian's fraught relationship with colonial violence and postcolonial struggles. In June 1960, the Republic of the Congo gained its independence from Belgium. Almost immediately, violence erupted between Congolese soldiers and the Belgian troops and civilians who remained in the former colony. The Belgian government responded to the unrest by deploying military forces to Congo. Seeking to quell tensions and end Belgian interference, Congolese Prime Minister Patrice Lumumba called on the United Nations to intervene with a peacekeeping force. The UN eventually deployed more than

twenty thousand military and civilian staff to Congo. It became
the largest UN peacekeeping mission during the Cold War era.

The UN intervention in Congo had explicit humanitarian aims:
to protect civilians from violence and support the delivery of
critically needed food and medical aid. Despite its stated goals, the
four-year mission bred significant controversy. High-ranking UN
officials, most of them western European, doubted the Congolese
people's capacity for self-government. UN peacekeepers therefore
extended significant authority over Congolese military,
governmental, and civil affairs. Many Congolese critics, in turn,
came to see the UN mission as an affront to their sovereignty,
perceiving peacekeeping as a new manifestation of colonialism.
Protests reached a fever pitch following Lumumba's assassination
in January 1961, with many accusing the UN of colluding with
Western governments to secure the prime minister's removal from
power. Congolese and international resentment over these events
fueled mounting critiques of UN peacekeeping missions—and the
international humanitarian system more broadly—in the
years ahead.

Global refugee crises posed an additional set of challenges for
the international humanitarian system. During the 1950s and
early 1960s, millions of people around the world became
displaced due to war, revolution, and political unrest. Following
the 1949 Chinese Communist Revolution, more than a million
people crossed the border into Hong Kong, then a British
colony. During the 1950s, hundreds of thousands fled the
violence of the Algerian Revolution, migrating into neighboring
Tunisia and Morocco. And in 1956, after the Soviet Union
cracked down on the Hungarian Revolution, 200,000 left
Hungary, seeking safety in neighboring Austria and Yugoslavia.
Although governments had recently negotiated a landmark set
of protections for refugees, the 1951 Refugee Convention, this
treaty applied only to Europeans who had fled their home
countries prior to 1951.

The absence of clear law or policy left humanitarian organizations scrambling to improvise assistance for Chinese, Algerian, and Hungarian refugees. In each case, the new Office of the UN High Commissioner for Refugees (UNHCR) assumed a primary role in coordinating relief and resettlement efforts. In Hungary and Algeria, it also partnered with the League of Red Cross Societies (LRCS) to administer camps, distribute food and clothing, and provide medical care. These actions established both the UNHCR and LRCS as crucial players in global migration and displacement issues. Their collective efforts not only helped to sustain many people but also established new precedents for future refugee crises.

Despite these achievements, many of the broader structural and legal forces that hindered assistance to displaced people remained unresolved. In 1959–60, the UN and more than sixty countries organized the World Refugee Year, a campaign to raise awareness about the enduring plight of displaced people around the world. Substantive changes, however, were slow to materialize. Eventually, in 1967, the UN General Assembly adopted the Protocol relating to the Status of Refugees. The 1967 Protocol extended the terms of the 1951 Refugee Convention to all populations "without any geographical limitation," intending to ensure that "the protection provided to refugees is more universal in scope." Though this reform marked a noteworthy achievement, the violence of the global Cold War and the upheaval of decolonization made population displacement an ongoing humanitarian challenge.

Even as they grappled with refugee crises, colonial conflicts, and proxy wars, humanitarians did not ignore peacetime concerns. During the 1950s and early 1960s, the LRCS significantly expanded its involvement in the field of international disaster assistance. While continuing to promote and coordinate the relief efforts of National Red Cross and Red Crescent Societies, the LRCS Secretariat began to send its own delegates to the scene of major disasters. The organization played a prominent role in multiple catastrophes, including flooding across India and Pakistan in 1954 and 1955, violent earthquakes in Chile in 1960 and Yugoslavia in 1963, and Hurricane Flora, which struck several Caribbean nations in 1963. These actions cemented the LRCS's reputation as a global authority in disaster management.

In many postcolonial and developing nations, humanitarian organizations administered a growing slate of long-term health and welfare projects, seeking to prevent suffering by tackling its root causes. Projects within the UN system illustrate just some of the burgeoning links between humanitarian relief and development assistance. The UN General Assembly first began apportioning funds for technical assistance projects during the late 1940s. As the number of UN member states increased due to decolonization, delegates from these new nations petitioned for more robust commitments to the developing world. As pressure grew, the General Assembly established a UN Special Fund for "the less developed countries" in 1958 and a new specialized agency, the UN Development Programme, in 1965. Additionally, the General Assembly proclaimed the 1960s "The Development Decade," spearheading a global campaign to improve living standards and eliminate hunger, disease, and illiteracy.

Many of the UN's specialized agencies also worked to address these issues. In 1960, the Food and Agriculture Organization (FAO) launched a "Freedom from Hunger Campaign," intended to promote public awareness and spur advocacy on the problem of global food insecurity. The following year, the General Assembly established the World Food Programme (WFP). Administered jointly by the UN and FAO, this multilateral organization was charged with coordinating emergency food relief operations. Within a few years, its staff delivered life-saving commodities to victims of famine in Sudan; an earthquake in Iran; tropical storms in Thailand, Haiti, and Cuba; and conflict in Algeria. Alongside these humanitarian activities, the WFP experimented with nutrition-related development projects. In 1963, its staff began this work with a school meals program in Togo and an agricultural development project in southern Egypt, laying foundations for similar initiatives elsewhere.

Other UN agencies targeted public health and disease. In 1948, pivoting away from postwar relief, the United Nations International Children's Emergency Fund (UNICEF) spearheaded a campaign to vaccinate children outside of Europe against tuberculosis. After it became a permanent UN agency in 1953, UNICEF continued to focus on improving child health and well-being globally. During the 1950s and early 1960s, it undertook programs to reduce childhood mortality by improving water supplies, sanitation, and nutrition. The World Health Organization (WHO), meanwhile, initiated ambitious crusades against infectious disease. In 1955, the WHO launched the Global Malaria Eradication Campaign, addressing one of the leading causes of death in sub-Saharan Africa, Southeast Asia, and South America. Four years later, it started the Smallpox Eradication Campaign, combatting one of the world's most lethal diseases through a combination of immunization and surveillance.

The UN system did not carry out these initiatives alone. Member governments financed the work of the WFP, the WHO, the UN Development Programme, and other agencies. Many states and voluntary organizations also administered their own technical and development assistance programs during the 1950s and 1960s. These assorted projects met with mixed success and some decisive failures. Nevertheless, they signaled a growing commitment to stemming humanitarian problems at their source.

Reckonings and turning points

By the mid-1960s, the international humanitarian system looked very different than it had just a generation prior. Between 1945 and 1963, thirty-two National Societies joined the International

Red Cross and Red Crescent Movement, the majority of them based in Asian and African countries, bringing its total membership to eighty-eight. The United Nations saw even greater membership growth, from 51 member states in 1945 to 113 in 1963. The UN system, now a central hub of humanitarian activities and agencies, was becoming more diverse in its representation. One year earlier, in 1962, a group of NGOs focused on refugees and migration joined together in Geneva to form the International Council of Voluntary Agencies, a new global network for nonstate humanitarian action. Multiple governments also established foreign aid offices during the early 1960s, including the French Ministries of Cooperation and External Affairs, the German Ministry of Development, the Japanese Overseas Technical Cooperation Agency, and the United States Agency for International Development (USAID).

The international humanitarian system was expanding—but not everyone considered that a good thing. By the mid-1960s, critiques of the world's dominant donor governments and humanitarian organizations were gaining currency within postcolonial nations, socialist countries, and left-wing political movements. Although aid workers from wealthy donor nations often presented humanitarian assistance as a liberal, internationalist mission to ameliorate human suffering, their critics held a different perspective. Humanitarian aid, they insisted, was merely a reinvention of colonial-era hierarchies. It allowed powerful states to maintain political and social control over former colonies, while perpetuating their economic dependence. States also employed humanitarian rhetoric to justify foreign interventions, critics noted, undermining postcolonial sovereignty and self-determination.

Humanitarianism's detractors extended many of these same arguments to international organizations, including the ICRC and LCRS, the UN's specialized agencies, and UN Peacekeeping forces. Though ostensibly international and multilateral, these institutions had long been dominated by North American and western European voices, personnel, and funding. In practice, they tended to align more closely with powerful Western countries than with socialist governments, national liberation movements, or postcolonial states. As a result, critics dismissed these organizations as pawns of imperial and capitalist interests.

In the face of such allegations, many humanitarians protested that their actions were wholly apolitical, motivated only by the purest of intentions. The most vigorous of these defenses emanated from the International Red Cross and Red Crescent Movement. In 1965, the ICRC, LRCS, and ninety-two National Societies proclaimed seven Fundamental Principles guiding all Red Cross action: humanity, impartiality, neutrality, independence, voluntary service, unity, and universality. The purpose of the Movement was "to protect life and health" and "to prevent and alleviate human suffering wherever it may be found." The Movement "may not take sides in hostilities," its leadership affirmed, and "makes no discrimination as to nationality, race, religious beliefs, class or political opinions." Though these principles originated within the International Red Cross and Red Crescent Movement, many other humanitarian organizations adopted a similar stance, pledging to remain above the fray of war and politics.

This proved exceedingly difficult, however. During the late 1960s and early 1970s, events in Vietnam, Nigeria, and East Pakistan (Bangladesh) prompted a reckoning within humanitarian circles, leading many to reconsider their positions on neutrality, impartiality, independence, and other core values.

The American War in Vietnam marked the first pivotal turning point. Like the Korean War before it, the Vietnam conflict was both a civil struggle over competing nationalist visions and a textbook proxy war. On one side was the South Vietnamese government and its chief ally, the United States, with support from Australia, New Zealand, the Philippines, Thailand, and several other countries. On the other was the North Vietnamese government and a South Vietnamese insurgency, the National Liberation Front, backed primarily by China and the Soviet Union. Caught in the middle were Vietnamese civilians. Millions became orphans and refugees during the brutal twenty-year conflict. Malnutrition, waterborne diseases, land mines, chemical burns, and mass bombing campaigns all contributed to widespread suffering in Vietnam, and eventually other parts of Indochina.

Allied countries funneled considerable humanitarian aid into the two Vietnams, in patterns that mirrored Cold War divisions. North Vietnam received food and medical supplies from China, the Soviet Union, and multiple Eastern Bloc countries. Medical missions from socialist nations ran clinics, built hospitals, and constructed equipment factories, establishing a local source for vaccines and surgical supplies. South Vietnam's Asian and Pacific allies, likewise, dispatched material relief and aid workers to that country. Its principal ally, the US government, relied heavily on the American voluntary sector to administer orphanages, health clinics, and refugee services. By 1970, thirty-three American voluntary organizations were operating humanitarian programs in South Vietnam. US officials also collaborated with these NGOs to pursue agricultural and technical development projects, pledging to eliminate "the hunger, disease, poverty and illiteracy upon which communism feeds."

Yet as violence escalated during the late 1960s and early 1970s, many American aid workers grew disillusioned. The US military's intensive bombing campaigns in North Vietnam, and in neighboring Cambodia and Laos, produced enormous civilian casualties. Although ICRC officials questioned whether these collateral damages were too excessive, they did not press the matter vigorously. By contrast, a global chorus of grass-roots antiwar protestors vocally criticized the US war effort, often condemning American NGOs for their complicity. Organizations

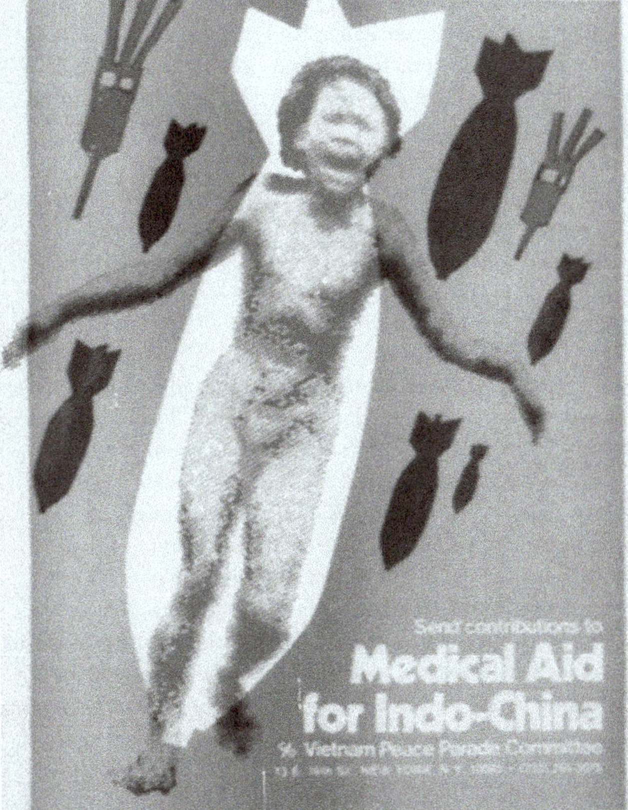

9. Together with events in Biafra and Bangladesh, the American War in Vietnam led many to rethink the traditional principles of humanitarianism, such as neutrality and impartiality. Others began to question the long tradition of state-private cooperation in humanitarian affairs.

like Catholic Relief Services and CARE, in turn, started to question the moral legitimacy of partnering with the US government. Were they helping perpetuate a humanitarian crisis rather than ameliorating it, their personnel wondered? Pacifist relief organizations like the American Friends Service Committee went even further. Its members openly protested the conduct of the war and, in an act of civil disobedience, illegally shipped aid supplies to North Vietnam.

By the time US forces withdrew from Vietnam in 1973, the postwar consensus on state-private humanitarianism had developed deep fissures. In the United States and elsewhere, voluntary agencies began demanding greater independence, asserting their identity as *non*governmental organizations.

In postcolonial West Africa, meanwhile, a second major challenge to humanitarian ideals and ethics was brewing. Soon after Nigeria achieved independence in 1960, political and ethno-religious violence started to escalate between the country's Hausa-Fulani and Igbo populations. Eventually, Igbo communities in southeastern Nigeria chose to secede, declaring independence in May 1967 as the Republic of Biafra. The Nigerian government, dominated by Hausa-Fulani interests, responded to Biafra's secession with a violent campaign to reunify the country. Nigerian authorities also imposed a blockade on Biafra, preventing food and medical supplies from entering the region. By the time Biafra fell in early 1970, between one and two million people had died from this policy of intentional starvation, most of them children and other civilians. Another ten million people became internally displaced.

International organizations struggled to respond to the spiraling humanitarian crisis in Biafra. Leaders within the UN system were reluctant to become involved, arguing that the UN's mandate did not include internal conflicts. Most notably, the UNHCR claimed its authority extended only to refugees who had crossed an international border, not to internally displaced people. Assuming its traditional role as a neutral intermediary, the ICRC attempted to negotiate with belligerents on both sides. After the Nigerian government refused access to the disputed region, however, ICRC leaders made a controversial decision: to defy the federal blockade and deliver provisions to Biafra via airlift. The Nigerian military responded to this unauthorized intervention by killing several Red Cross workers and shooting down an ICRC plane. Shaken by these experiences, ICRC leaders suspended further relief flights and strove to reclaim their neutral position.

Rejecting the cautious stance of UN agencies, the ICRC, and their own governments, voluntary relief agencies dominated the humanitarian response to the Biafra crisis. Widely covered by the international media, the famine in Biafra became a cause-célèbre throughout Europe and North America. NGOs like Oxfam and Save the Children tapped into this public outrage to mobilize mass support for Biafran relief efforts. Joint Church Aid, a coalition of faith-based agencies from thirty-three countries, supplemented the ICRC's airlift with an airlift of its own. Its personnel flew food and medical supplies into Biafra throughout the duration of the conflict, helping sustain millions of civilians behind the blockade. The Biafran emergency marked a defining moment for the voluntary sector, with NGOs assuming a more central and assertive position in the humanitarian sphere.

Yet at the same time, the Nigerian Civil War sparked fierce debates over core humanitarian principles, sowing deep divisions within the aid community. The International Red Cross and Red Crescent Movement had long held its neutrality paramount. Remaining neutral was essential to retain the confidence of belligerents, proponents argued, ensuring access to all victims of conflict. While volunteering in Nigeria, a pair of young French doctors—Bernard Kouchner and Max Récamier—developed a different perspective. Humanitarians, they came to believe, had a responsibility to bear witness to atrocities and speak out against them. The welfare of survivors, they insisted, must take priority over political neutrality or respect for sovereign borders. Three years later, Kouchner and Récamier joined with other like-minded French physicians and surgeons to establish Médecins Sans Frontières (MSF, Doctors Without Borders), a new type of humanitarian NGO grounded in these alternate principles.

A fierce debate had split the aid community: should humanitarians strive to be apolitical, or should they embrace the notion that humanitarian action was innately political? Disagreements over this issue continued to percolate.

Shortly after the fall of Biafra, a series of successive crises in South Asia further reoriented international humanitarianism. When Pakistan became a nation-state in 1947, it originally comprised two noncontiguous regions, East and West Pakistan. Relations between them were already strained when, in November 1970, the Bhola Cyclone smashed into East Pakistan, killing between 300,000 and 500,000 people. The central government's lackluster response to this catastrophe catalyzed demands for independence among East Pakistan's majority Bengali population. In March 1971, the military government in West Pakistan met these calls with a brutal campaign of mass murder and rape, resulting in hundreds of thousands of casualties. The people of East Pakistan fought back, in what became known as the Bangladesh Liberation War. They ultimately won independence in December 1971, becoming the new nation of Bangladesh.

Bangladeshi independence came at the cost of a staggering humanitarian crisis, arising from the concomitant effects of natural hazard, genocide, and war. Nearly ten million people in East Pakistan fled into neighboring India during 1971, creating the largest refugee crisis since the Second World War. The Indian government responded to the situation by organizing food distribution centers and more than eight hundred camps. The vast influx of people, however, quickly overwhelmed these facilities.

Sanitary conditions deteriorated, leading to outbreaks of cholera, dysentery, and other deadly diseases. In late April 1971, Indian authorities appealed for international assistance to supplement their efforts, insisting that the refugees were "clearly the responsibility of the World Community."

In contrast to its heel-dragging over Biafra, the UNHCR assumed a prominent role in this transborder crisis. For the first time, it became the general coordinator, or focal point, for all UN assistance. Its staff worked with the WFP, WHO, and UNICEF to procure and deliver commodities, medicines, vaccines, and other vital supplies to India. UNHCR also promoted international fundraising efforts and liaised with Indian authorities, foreign governments, and NGOs. After Bangladesh won its independence, the agency oversaw the repatriation process, helping to resettle nine million people by March 1972.

NGOs again played a prominent role in the Bangladesh crisis and its aftermath. Personnel from Oxfam, CARE, Save the Children, and other agencies became a visible presence in Indian refugee camps, where they operated programs of food and medical relief. Yet once the fighting ended, foreign aid workers did not depart. As refugees returned home, many NGOs followed in their footsteps, shifting their energies from humanitarian relief to development projects. In postwar Bangladesh, NGOs established a vast web of housing, healthcare, agricultural, and technical assistance programs. Although many welcomed this aid, the indeterminate presence of foreign aid workers also bred considerable resentment. So did the paternalism, condescension, and racial and cultural insensitivity that many aid workers exhibited. In the eyes of Bangladeshi critics, the ballooning NGO sector in their new nation represented just another expression of Western colonialism.

Together, events in Vietnam, Biafra, and Bangladesh pushed humanitarianism in new directions. By the mid-1970s, many aid workers had begun to reassess their relationships to politics, to governments, and to one another. The aid sector was becoming an entrenched fixture in many developing nations, a pattern critics decried as neocolonialism. Yet at the same time, formerly colonized states were exercising greater sway in humanitarian governance, challenging the prerogatives of more powerful countries. Throughout the late Cold War era, these trends remained deeply influential.

An era of increasing complexity

Amid the soul-searching of the 1970s, efforts to improve the international humanitarian system found fertile soil. Throughout the decade, states and international organizations made significant reforms in several key areas, including disaster assistance and the laws of war. Compromises made along the way, however, limited their potential impacts.

During the 1970s, the human and financial toll of disasters was on the rise. Droughts, floods, tropical storms, earthquakes, and other natural hazards affected an estimated forty-four million people annually, most of them in lower-income nations. Vulnerability to disasters increased for many reasons, including population growth, urbanization in hazard-prone areas, and ecological stresses like deforestation and erosion. No matter the cause, the proliferation of deadly and costly disasters created serious concern. Although donor nations, NGOs, and the LRCS regularly contributed assistance following major catastrophes, this aid increasingly proved insufficient, especially as the costs of relief and recovery soared.

Within the UN General Assembly and the UN Economic and Social Council (ECOSOC), pressure began building for a specialized UN disaster assistance agency and a permanent, multilateral disaster aid fund. First surfacing during the mid-1960s, demands for these initiatives intensified in 1970 and

1971, following a catastrophic earthquake in Peru and the Bhola Cyclone in East Pakistan. Leading this campaign were delegates from hazard-prone lower-income nations, including Algeria, Chile, Cuba, India, Iraq, Pakistan, and Turkey. The existing international machinery for disaster relief, they stressed, was unreliable and inadequate. Noting that disasters posed a particular obstacle for lower-income and postcolonial nations, they also called for disaster planning to be incorporated into development programs.

This campaign for improved international action in disaster assistance achieved mixed success. Powerful states and many international organizations opposed the establishment of either a brand-new humanitarian agency or a permanent emergency fund. As a compromise, the General Assembly created a more limited entity, the Office of the United Nations Disaster Relief Coordinator (UNDRO), in late 1971. UNDRO's mandate was to coordinate the disaster relief activities of existing UN agencies. It also served as a liaison with the LRCS, governments, and voluntary organizations. Finally, the new office was charged with promoting international disaster prevention and preparedness activities. UNDRO's establishment marked a concrete step toward multilateral cooperation in disaster management. However, an unclear mandate, limited funding, and tensions with other agencies all hampered its effectiveness. UNDRO was roundly criticized for its lackluster response to multiple disasters, including the 1972 Managua earthquake, the Sahel drought and famine of the early 1970s, and the 1976 Guatemala City earthquake. All the while, the risks and destructive consequences of natural hazards continued to escalate.

As UNDRO floundered in the mid-1970s, a movement to revise international humanitarian law was gaining steam. Since the adoption of the 1949 Geneva Conventions, the nature of warfare had changed dramatically. Internal conflicts became far more common than wars between nation-states. Anticolonial liberation wars, conducted with guerilla-style tactics and brutal counterinsurgency campaigns, further changed the character of hostilities. Together, these types of conflicts exposed glaring gaps in international humanitarian law. The 1949 Geneva Conventions, critics maintained, did not do enough to protect civilian populations from harm. Their applicability to non-international conflicts remained ill-defined, and their place in national liberation wars was hotly contested.

Calls to address these issues first arose in the UN General Assembly during the late 1960s. Taking up the issue, the ICRC drafted a pair of Additional Protocols to the Geneva Conventions. Delegates from 155 nations then convened in Geneva to negotiate these new accords, meeting in four sessions from 1974 to 1977. After acrimonious debate and significant compromises, they eventually adopted the two Additional Protocols in 1977.

Additional Protocol I pertained to international conflicts. It created new protections for civilians and prisoners of war, and it established new rules for conducting warfare. It enshrined the principle of proportionality, stipulating that any incidental harm to civilians must not be excessive in relation to anticipated military advantage. Crucially, it also expanded the definition of interstate conflicts to include wars "against colonial domination and alien occupation and against racist régimes." Wealthy Western powers like France and the United States vigorously opposed this measure. However, a coalition of postcolonial and socialist countries successfully lobbied for its inclusion. Through their pressure, international humanitarian law broadened to encompass wars of self-determination, a significant innovation.

Additional Protocol II expanded the essential rules of war to internal conflicts, building on Common Article 3 of the 1949 Geneva Conventions. Multiple states objected to the initial drafts of this treaty. Opponents argued it would prevent governments from maintaining law and order within their own borders. They also deemed it a threat to state sovereignty, warning it would be used to justify foreign interventions. Bowing to these protests, delegates eventually agreed to a pared-down version of Protocol II. Though it covered a narrower range of internal conflicts and fewer protected categories than originally proposed, this treaty nevertheless represented another key development in international humanitarian law.

Both UNDRO and the Additional Protocols were intended to strengthen humanitarian protections for victims of disaster and war. The success of these efforts remained to be seen. During the late 1970s and 1980s, crises around the world repeatedly tested the international humanitarian system. They underscored just how difficult it remained to prevent and alleviate human suffering.

One of the greatest humanitarian crises of the late Cold War era occurred in Cambodia, Vietnam's neighbor to the west. In 1975, after years of civil war and upheaval, a radical communist movement called the Khmer Rouge seized power in Cambodia. The worst was yet to come. Over the next four years, the revolutionary regime killed two million Cambodians—a quarter of the population—via mass executions, starvation, and disease. Eventually, the Vietnamese military invaded Cambodia and overthrew the Khmer Rouge, replacing it with a pro-Vietnamese government in early 1979. Fighting continued, however, pitting Vietnamese occupiers against the remnants of the Khmer Rouge. On the heels of genocide, famine and armed conflict now gripped Cambodia. Fleeing the unrest, hundreds of thousands of Cambodian refugees congregated on the border of Thailand, in camps controlled mainly by Khmer Rouge forces.

As awareness of the famine and refugee crisis grew in 1979, many international aid organizations attempted to intervene. Cambodian authorities, backed by Vietnam, tentatively agreed to accept external assistance. However, they were determined to keep that aid out of enemy hands. To that end, they demanded control over the distribution of food and other supplies. They also refused to permit relief activities on the Thai-Cambodian border, where the Khmer Rouge remained dominant. These conditions posed a profound dilemma: they required aid agencies to sacrifice their principles of neutrality and impartiality in exchange for gaining access to sufferers.

These proposed requirements split the aid community, reigniting debates over humanitarian ethics and best practices. Oxfam's leaders chose to accept the Cambodian government's conditions. Oxfam went on to lead a consortium of thirty-one European NGOs, delivering food to starving civilians within Cambodia while largely ignoring refugees on the Thai border. Other aid agencies opted to bypass the Cambodian government entirely and funneled aid to refugee camps on the Thai-Cambodian border. UNHRC and the WFP together coordinated a major international aid operation within the contested region. By late 1980, sixty European and American NGOs were also conducting relief programs on the border. Taking yet another approach, the ICRC and UNICEF initially repudiated the government's conditions. However, they eventually brokered a compromise with Cambodian authorities, negotiating partial access to both famine victims and refugees. The two organizations went on to undertake a Joint Mission in Cambodia. It grew into one of the largest relief operations in the ICRC's history.

The problem of access, it turned out, was only the first hurdle. On the ground, humanitarian organizations experienced numerous additional frustrations. Both Khmer Rouge forces and Cambodian and Vietnamese authorities confiscated much of the international aid, channeling food and other supplies toward their respective soldiers and political allies. Combatants repeatedly attacked and ransacked refugee camps, adding to the plight of their inhabitants. Amid mounting reports of misconduct and corruption, most major aid organizations withdrew from Cambodia by the early 1980s, just a few years after arriving. Conflict, however, dragged on for another decade. Tens of thousands of Cambodians remained in refugee camps until as late as 1993.

The Cambodian crisis became another critical moment for the humanitarian sector. It revealed the ethical and logistical challenges of operating in conflicts whose belligerents flouted the laws of war. A concurrent emergency in the Horn of Africa proved equally consequential, further underscoring the political impediments to humanitarian action during the late Cold War era.

Between 1983 and 1985, a severe famine occurred in Ethiopia. At least 600,000 people died during these years from malnutrition-related diseases and starvation, while 400,000 fled the country as refugees, and another 2.5 million people became internally displaced. Although a drought was partly to blame for local crop failures, the famine in Ethiopia—like all modern famines—was primarily attributable to human actions and inaction.

The emergency in Ethiopia was a creeping disaster, not a sudden crisis. In 1974, after years of rising instability, a revolutionary junta called the Dergue deposed Ethiopian emperor Haile Selassie and installed a Marxist-Leninist dictatorship. Supported by the Soviet Union, the Dergue imposed a slate of radical reforms, which included the forced collectivization of Ethiopian agriculture. Such policies ignited considerable opposition, giving rise to armed insurgencies and secessionist movements. The Dergue responded with harsh counterinsurgency measures, including the destruction of crops and livestock, intentionally constricting the food supply. By the early 1980s, the government's agricultural and military policies had already created widespread food shortages in Ethiopia. The onset of a long, intense period of drought exacerbated this situation. By the winter of 1983–84, food insecurity spiraled into a full-scale famine.

Outside Ethiopia, human choices further shaped the developing crisis. Plenty of surplus food existed elsewhere in the world. A lack of international awareness and political will, however, impeded humanitarian agencies from delivering it—until late 1984, that is, when the situation abruptly changed. In October, BBC News aired a televised report on the famine, featuring graphic images of emaciated children and grieving mothers. Similar coverage quickly spread within other countries. Overnight, the Ethiopian famine became *the* global cause. Within a few months, dozens of A-list musicians recorded chart-topping singles such as "Do They Know It's Christmas" and "We Are the World," imploring listeners to "feed the world." Donations to NGOs soared, and citizens of many countries called on their governments to act. In July 1985, 1.5 billion people in 150 countries tuned in for a televised fundraising concert called Live Aid. The event raised an astonishing $140,000,000 for famine relief.

Although mass media and celebrity spectacles galvanized international support for famine sufferers, these popular appeals carried many negative repercussions. For one, they depoliticized the crisis, portraying it as a natural disaster while erasing its human causes. They advanced a patronizing and stereotypical narrative, in which "white saviors" rescued generic "Africans" from their misery. Relying on lurid, degrading imagery of starving and dead Ethiopian people, they undermined respect for human dignity. Finally, they perpetuated racialized depictions of Africa as a failed continent, defined solely by poverty, conflict, and chronic hunger. In coming years, critical awareness of these issues prompted the aid sector to rethink the ethics of representing human suffering.

Yet at the time, humanitarian organizations were focused on one thing: channeling the flood of donations they received into tangible assistance. Between late 1984 and 1986, large quantities of food and medical supplies arrived in Ethiopia. International aid came via UN agencies like UNDRO, the WFP, and UNICEF. The LRCS and dozens of NGOs contributed, too, as did many state agencies. A staggering one-third of all private and public aid came from the US government. Guided by Cold War geopolitics, US officials used famine relief to discredit Ethiopia's socialist government and its principal ally, the Soviet Union, seeking to score diplomatic points for their own country.

To the chagrin of many foreign aid workers, these international assistance efforts quickly became embroiled in the Dergue's counterinsurgency operations. Placing stringent requirements on foreign NGOs, the Ethiopian government delegated considerable control over food distributions to the nation's Relief and Rehabilitation Commission. Government authorities requisitioned donated commodities to feed their troops and reward supporters. They also prevented much food aid from reaching the rebelling northern provinces, where famine conditions were most severe. Additionally, the Dergue took advantage of the camps and feeding centers that international organizations ran, using these sites as transit points in its forced resettlement campaigns. In late 1985, the president of Médecins Sans Frontières spoke out against these abuses, condemning the Dergue for manipulating humanitarian assistance. Ethiopian authorities responded by expelling MSF from the country. Most other agencies kept quiet, choosing not to jeopardize their access—however circumscribed—to famine sufferers.

In Ethiopia, as in Cambodia, aid organizations confronted the fraught relationship between humanitarianism, war, disaster, and politics. But these episodes were hardly anomalous. Throughout the late 1970s and 1980s, similar challenges, complications, and controversies arose amid numerous other crises. They included civil wars in Guatemala, El Salvador, Lebanon, and Mozambique; catastrophic earthquakes in Tangshan, China, Mexico City, and Armenia; and prolonged conflicts between Iran and Iraq, and the Soviet Union and Afghanistan.

A growing proportion of these crises stemmed from multiple causes, including armed violence, natural hazards, and underdevelopment. They also had multiple dimensions, including food insecurity, population displacement, ethno-religious or political persecution, and the disruption of medical and social systems. Toward the end of the 1980s, a new term began gaining currency within the aid sector to describe these sorts of multilayered events. Increasingly, practitioners operated in a world of "complex humanitarian emergencies."

It was not only crises that had become more complicated. By the early 1990s, the entire humanitarian system had grown vastly more complex. In the half-century since the Second World War, the aid sector had ballooned in size. It now comprised hundreds of intergovernmental organizations, NGOs, and state agencies. A diverse range of voices and perspectives now influenced humanitarian governance. Relief, recovery, and development had grown more entangled. As the global Cold War ended and the era of decolonization closed, the international humanitarian sector turned its attention to the challenges and possibilities of a dawning millennium.

Chapter 6
Humanitarianism in flux

In the 1990s, the word "new" seemed ubiquitous. As the decade commenced, the Cold War's end elicited jubilant pronouncements of a "new world order," guided by commitments to peace, justice, multilateralism, and collective security. By the late 1990s, this optimism had been tarnished by repeated instances of armed violence, terrorism, human rights violations, and mass atrocities. Grappling with these events, analysts began speaking of "new wars," whose actors, goals, and tactics distinguished them from conventional conflicts. Around the world, people awaited the year 2000 with a mixture of hope and trepidation, reflecting on the complex challenges facing global humanity in the new millennium.

In this context, talk of a "new humanitarianism" became increasingly influential within the aid sector. If the "old humanitarianism" was supposed to privilege the neutral delivery of life-saving emergency relief, the new humanitarianism was defined by very different principles and objectives. In addition to the alleviation of human suffering, it encompassed the defense of human rights, the pursuit of long-term development work, and the promotion of peacebuilding. Proponents of the new humanitarianism also embraced a more politically conscious approach. Aid workers must sometimes choose sides and advocate for victims of atrocity, they insisted, rejecting the idea that humanitarians must always remain neutral.

In fact, none of this was truly novel. The defining attributes of the "new humanitarianism" had begun to coalesce during the previous few decades, while some of its antecedents stretched back even further. Around the turn of the twenty-first century, however, this constellation of principles and practices became increasingly mainstream. Since that time, these ideas have transformed the aid sector. Many have embraced the new humanitarianism as a better model for the new millennium. However, it has also generated pushback. When aid became overtly politicized, critics warned, humanitarians risked losing access to suffering populations. The emphasis on human rights, development assistance, and peacebuilding, they cautioned, came at the expense of humanitarianism's most fundamental priorities: saving lives, reducing acute suffering, and meeting peoples' basic needs.

Since the 1990s, debate over these issues has persisted and the "new" humanitarianism has continued to evolve, adapting in response to contemporary crises. In the twenty-first century, the number of people affected by humanitarian emergencies has risen precipitously, dramatically increasing global need. Crises have become more complex and enduring, involving a potent mix of internal and transborder conflict, mass displacement, ethno-religious and political persecution, and environmental destruction. More and more, the impacts of climate change are compounding these factors. Today, the climate crisis ranks as one of the world's most pressing humanitarian concerns.

Amid this precarity, the international humanitarian system has swelled, growing into a multibillion-dollar global industry. Its expansion has not occurred without controversy, however. Since the 1990s, the humanitarian sector has weathered a barrage of internal and external criticisms, directed toward aid workers, donor governments and organizations, and the entire aid ecosystem. But these critiques have also inspired some earnest and encouraging reform efforts, designed to make aid more efficacious, accountable, and responsive to the needs of local actors. Today's humanitarianism is a product of these collective developments.

The entangling of humanitarianism and human rights

The new humanitarianism stemmed from a confluence of events, ideas, and political and cultural forces. It had no single source. That said, two crises during the 1990s were especially pivotal to the rise of this new paradigm.

One of them was the 1994 genocide in Rwanda. Rooted in a civil war between the country's Hutu ethnic majority and Tutsi minority population, the Rwandan genocide transpired during the uneasy peace that followed. On April 7, 1994, Hutu extremists launched a campaign of ethnic cleansing against Tutsis and moderate Hutus. Over the next hundred days, they slaughtered some 800,000 people. Roughly 2,500 UN Peacekeepers were stationed in Rwanda when the killing began. They did little to intervene, however, and the UN Security Council swiftly withdrew most of them. A commitment to neutrality, uncertainty over the permissible use of force, and a justified fear of retaliation all contributed to the UN's inaction. But the UN was not alone. Initially, many states and NGOs were highly reluctant to become involved in Rwanda, despite full knowledge of the atrocities.

As the bloodshed intensified, pressure for an international intervention eventually grew. In mid-May, the UN Security Council agreed to deploy five thousand Peacekeeping troops to Rwanda. It also authorized a French-led military operation, Opération Turquoise, charged with establishing a humanitarian safe zone in the country. Foreign forces did not arrive until late June, however, after most of the killings had already occurred.

While supporters of Opération Turquoise claim that it saved tens of thousands of Tutsi lives, moreover, critics accused the French military of aiding the Hutu extremists who were responsible for the genocide and helping them seek refuge across the border.

The genocide finally ended in early July, when a Tutsi-dominated rebel movement took control over Rwanda. In its wake, many condemned the international community for its inertia and indifference. Haunted by the failure to prevent or stop the mass killings, voices within the aid sector vowed to act differently in the next crisis.

The next crisis, it turns out, was already in the making. Since 1991, interlinked ethno-religious and civil conflicts had been raging in the Balkans, known collectively as the Yugoslav Wars. The fighting was especially intense in Bosnia and Herzegovina, where it embroiled ethnic Serbs, ethnic Croats, and Bosniaks (Bosnian Muslims), as well as the Serbian-dominated Yugoslav military. Serb-controlled forces unleashed a campaign of ethnic cleansing against Bosniaks, perpetrating mass rapes, forced displacement, and other war crimes. By the time the Bosnian War ended in November 1995, more than 100,000 people had died, the majority of them Bosniaks. Roughly 2.6 million were displaced, either internally or as refugees in other countries.

The conflict in Bosnia and Herzegovina presented one of the first major tests for the international humanitarian system after the Cold War. The UNHCR coordinated a major humanitarian operation in the region, collaborating with the ICRC, the WFP, and more than 250 NGOs to execute it. Together, they administered a massive airlift of food and other aid to Sarajevo and distributed 950,000 tons of supplies throughout the region. Supporting these initiatives, the UN Security Council deployed forces to protect the flow of aid into the Sarajevo airport. It also established six "safe areas" under the protection of UN

Peacekeepers, meant to shield civilians from attack and ensure their access to humanitarian assistance.

These efforts helped meet the basic needs of millions of civilians, yet they did little to circumvent the mass atrocities responsible for so much of the war's suffering. The UN safe areas, though ostensibly humanitarian spaces, were overcrowded, poorly resourced, and under constant state of siege. These failures became painfully evident in July 1995, when the Bosnian Serb army advanced on the town of Srebrenica, a designated UN safe area. Four hundred UN Peacekeepers were stationed in Srebrenica, but they were outnumbered and quickly overtaken. They stood by as Serb forces summarily executed eight thousand Bosnian Muslim men and boys. The international community's impotence during the Srebrenica massacre—later ruled a genocide—left many wondering whether humanitarians had learned any lessons from Rwanda at all.

Although the Bosnian War ended in 1995, violence resumed in the Balkans in early 1998, when ethnic Albanians in the province of Kosovo rose up against Serbian rule. Once again, the Serbian-dominated Yugoslav government responded with violent repression and attacks on civilians. This time, however, the North Atlantic Treaty Organization (NATO) intervened with military force. In March 1999, NATO launched a campaign of air strikes in Kosovo and Serbia. After seventy-eight days of bombing, Serbian president Slobodan Milošević agreed to withdraw from Kosovo and allow international administration of the province.

NATO's actions in Kosovo proved highly controversial. NATO leadership defended the bombing campaign as a humanitarian intervention, carried out to prevent mass atrocities and ethnic cleansing. Rejecting this justification, critics condemned NATO for acting without UN authorization and violating Serbian sovereignty. The air strikes produced roughly two thousand civilian casualties and destroyed many nonmilitary targets, stoking further outrage. In critics' eyes, the bombing campaign was not a humanitarian operation; it was a gross violation of international humanitarian law.

As the twenty-first century dawned, experiences in Rwanda, the Balkans, and other complex emergencies influenced a pair of notable shifts, both central in forging the "new humanitarianism." First, they fueled the rise of what is called a "rights-based approach" to humanitarianism. This model emphasizes the necessity of upholding fundamental human rights during times of crisis. Grounded in the 1948 Universal Declaration of Human Rights and other international covenants, this encompasses the rights to be free from torture, forced labor, arbitrary arrest, and ethnic and religious discrimination. It also includes the right to seek asylum from persecution and the right to food, water, shelter, and medical care in times of need. Going beyond palliative care, rights-based humanitarianism targets the political causes of suffering. Additionally, it aims to empower survivors to assert their inalienable rights. Though precursors to this approach first appeared during the 1970s and 1980s, rights-based language became far more commonplace during the 1990s, a trend that has continued into this century.

Second, the crises of the 1990s ignited fierce debates over the ethics and legality of "humanitarian interventions": the use of cross-border military force to prevent mass atrocities and halt human rights abuses. In 2000, UN Secretary-General Kofi Annan asked, "How should we respond to a Rwanda, to a Srebrenica, to gross and systematic violations of human rights that offend every precept of our common humanity?" A decisive answer to Annan's question came in the form of a 2001 report entitled *The Responsibility to Protect.* Produced by an ad-hoc international commission, the report rejected the principle that national sovereignty is absolute. States, the commission argued, bear the primary responsibility for the welfare of their own populations. But when a government fails to protect its citizens—or actively perpetrates atrocities against them—then the international community has the right and the obligation to intervene. Though peaceful interventions through diplomatic channels should always take precedence, the commission concluded, coercive military force was permissible as a last resort.

Four years later, at the 2005 United Nations World Summit, UN Member States unanimously endorsed these principles, formally accepting the "Responsibility to Protect" (R2P) as an international norm. With this vote, world leaders avowed their shared responsibility to protect people from genocide, war crimes, ethnic cleansing, and crimes against humanity. They also affirmed the UN Security Council's power to authorize collective military interventions for humanitarian ends.

While many view the R2P doctrine as a positive development, some of its aspects have proven quite contentious. One central critique is that R2P infringes too far on the sovereignty and internal affairs of nation-states, undermining an established cornerstone of international relations. Another major criticism is that it promotes overly militarized solutions to humanitarian problems. The use of coercive and destructive military force, detractors insist, risks further destabilizing societies that are already in crisis, thus doing more harm than good. Still other critics denounce R2P as a cover for regime change and a front for neo-imperialism, decrying it as a moral fig leaf for major powers to invade other nations. Even those who accept the doctrine in principle often disagree on what situations justify its implementation in practice. Despite these assorted critiques and challenges, R2P has been invoked in more than eighty UN Security Council resolutions. It has become an influential (if imperfect) international norm.

Complex emergencies, complex responses

By the dawn of the new millennium in 2001, humanitarianism and human rights were becoming deeply entangled. Over the next twenty years, they continued to intertwine, informing the aid sector's actions in war zones, post-conflict situations, and other states of emergency. During the first two decades of the twenty-first century, humanitarianism also intersected more closely with international development and peacebuilding. Though the lines between these categories often blurred in the past, by 2021 they had become especially porous.

What accounts for humanitarianism's increased convergence with development, peacebuilding, and human rights? While the conflicts in Rwanda and the Balkans offer partial clues, much of the explanation lies in the rising frequency of complex emergencies during the early twenty-first century. These crises stem from a combination of factors, including armed conflict, natural hazards, and political instability. They produce widespread human suffering and death and large numbers of affected and displaced civilians. They involve the protracted breakdown of political, social, and economic order, enduring for years and even decades. The impacts of climate change exacerbate these problems. Food insecurity triggered by drought or excess rainfall, displacement spurred by sea-level rise or destructive superstorms, and conflicts rooted in resource and water scarcity are among the many humanitarian consequences of the climate crisis.

As complex emergencies multiplied during the early 2000s, many within the aid sector came to view short-term relief as an insufficient response to human suffering. In addition to meeting basic needs, they wanted to secure more sustainable improvements in people's lives. They aspired to address the underlying causes of vulnerability, including poverty, inequality, food insecurity, and environmental shocks. They sought to reduce violence by working to prevent conflicts, resolve disputes diplomatically, and foster the conditions for a durable peace. To achieve these interconnected goals, humanitarians strengthened their collaborations with practitioners in other sectors and aligned their programming with other agencies. Along with "rights-based humanitarianism," terms such as "developmental relief" and the "humanitarian-development-peace nexus" entered the aid ecosystem's lexicon, reflecting the integration of once distinct fields.

A decisive moment in this process of convergence was the terrorist attacks of September 11, 2001, which opened a new chapter in humanitarianism's history. Less than a month after 9/11, US-led coalition forces invaded Afghanistan in pursuit of the group responsible for the attacks, al-Qaeda, and the Taliban-led government that harbored them. What began as a more focused mission in Afghanistan rapidly spiraled into a "Global War on Terror," an amorphous and sprawling campaign to eradicate terrorist activity everywhere. Its next major salvo was a controversial US-led invasion of Iraq in March 2003, premised on shaky claims that the Iraqi government possessed weapons of mass destruction. Over the next two decades, the fight against terrorism underpinned military operations in Libya, Pakistan, Syria, Somalia, Yemen, and other countries. Official combat missions also continued in Afghanistan and Iraq (with a three-year hiatus) until 2021. With no clear conditions for how it will end, the Global War on Terror remains an entrenched part of international relations to this day.

Whatever one's views on its merits or failings, the Global War on Terror came with staggering humanitarian costs. By 2023, an estimated 940,000 people had been killed by direct violence in Afghanistan, Iraq, and other post-9/11 conflicts. Nearly four million more died from indirect war-related causes, like illness or malnutrition. At least thirty-eight million people became internally displaced or fled across borders as refugees.

The destruction of hospitals, housing, and other infrastructure amplified these problems, as did the disruption of food, water, and electricity supplies. For innumerable people, the twenty-first century has thus far passed in a perpetual state of emergency.

Between 2001 and 2021, the world's major aid agencies spent billions of dollars trying to address this widespread suffering. Despite these efforts, numerous obstacles stood in the way of effective humanitarian action. One major impediment was the politicization of humanitarian aid, both real and perceived. Shortly after the 2001 invasion of Afghanistan, US Secretary of State Colin Powell publicly praised American NGOs as a "force multiplier" in the fight against terrorism, calling them "an important part of our combat team." The implication that aid agencies had taken sides in the war on terror stood in direction contradiction to the humanitarian principles of neutrality and independence. While many agencies staunchly defended their autonomy, others saw legitimate reasons to collaborate. The US government and its allies justified their actions in Afghanistan and Iraq as humanitarian interventions, citing the Taliban's oppression of women and girls, torture and persecution of civilians by Iraqi authorities, and other human rights abuses as a rationale for involvement. In the United States and elsewhere, some aid organizations concurred with these justifications—at least initially—and became willing partners of warring states.

Whether or not they maintained an independent stance, the perception that aid workers had forsaken neutrality bred considerable distrust, with dangerous consequences. In 2003, a truck bomb exploded at the UN's headquarters in Baghdad, killing twenty-two people and wounding more than a hundred. From that point forward, politically motivated assassinations of aid workers steadily multiplied, imperiling operations in Afghanistan, Iraq, Somalia, Sudan, and other sites. In addition to heightening security risks, suspicion of aid workers led government officials and nonstate militias to interfere with humanitarian activities, blocking access to populations in need. In Nigeria, for example, government officials forced several NGOs to close their regional offices in 2019, accusing them of aiding jihadists and other opposition forces. Moreover, they only permitted NGOs to operate in areas dominated by the Nigerian military, preventing an estimated 800,000 people from receiving life-saving aid. Comparable scenes unfolded in multiple other countries during the early 2000s, creating considerable barriers to humanitarian action.

The indefinite duration and global scope of the post-9/11 wars posed a second significant challenge. Rather than achieving a stable peace, foreign interventions and anti-terrorist campaigns sparked a potent backlash. Militant insurgencies arose in multiple places, among them the Islamic State (ISIS), Boko Haram, offshoots of al-Qaeda, and a resurgent Taliban. The consequences were chronic political instability, sectarian violence, and ongoing conflict, including entrenched civil wars in both Afghanistan and Iraq. These issues compounded and prolonged humanitarian needs. In addition to providing short-term assistance, aid workers grappled with the effects of long-term displacement on affected populations, who lacked access to routine healthcare, mental health services, and formal education. As needs widened, the costs and complexity of addressing them spiraled. Yet as crises dragged on, public interest and funding for them also declined, a phenomenon known as "donor fatigue." Given these dynamics, it perhaps comes as little surprise that in early 2023 the UN reported that "Afghanistan remains the world's largest humanitarian crisis." With endless war came endless humanitarianism.

Not limited to Afghanistan and Iraq, drawn-out civil wars and chronic political violence gripped multiple countries during the early 2000s. Although the Global War on Terror was one important driver of conflict, many of these crises stemmed primarily from domestic and regional tensions. In Sudan, for instance, a brutal civil war raged from 1983 to 2005, propelled by the central government's marginalization of ethnic and religious minorities, competition over land and oil resources, and other grievances. Although the independence of South Sudan in 2011 created hope for peace, the next decade brought a six-year civil war to the new nation and a resurgence of conflict in Sudan itself. In 2011, civil war also erupted in Syria. The conflict was initially rooted in internal factors, including drought and agricultural failures, poverty and unemployment, anger over governmental corruption and repression, and the Syrian regime's crackdown on pro-democracy protests. Yet as the war dragged on, its dynamics shifted due to the involvement of external players, including the Islamic State (ISIS), Russia, Turkey, and the United States. In late 2024, after thirteen bloody years of fighting, a coalition of rebel groups ultimately ousted Syria's autocratic government, led by Bashar al-Assad. A more formal settlement, however, remained elusive.

Sudan and Syria were not alone. The Central African Republic, the Democratic Republic of Congo, Ethiopia, Libya, and Yemen all experienced lengthy civil wars during the early 2000s, some of which are still ongoing. In the Western Hemisphere, protracted crises affected multiple countries, including Colombia, El Salvador, Guatemala, Honduras, and Venezuela. Though these nations avoided descending into large-scale civil wars, issues such as gang-related violence, human rights abuses, high poverty rates, and the growing threat of natural hazards imperiled millions of lives.

All told, between 2001 and 2021, civil conflicts and chronic armed violence produced entrenched patterns of humanitarian need in dozens of countries. Millions of people died during these years as a result of war-related injuries, starvation, disease, genocide, and ethnic cleansing. Tragic as these figures are, the number of civilians dying as a result of wartime violence was proportionally much *lower* than it had been during the twentieth century. But this silver lining came with a tradeoff: skyrocketing levels of need among survivors. In 2021 alone, an estimated 306 million people required humanitarian assistance globally. Protracted crises, lasting at least five consecutive years, affected thirty-six countries. During 2021, more than eighty-six million people across the globe were also forcibly displaced. Having fled their homes due to armed conflict or persecution, these populations now experienced socioeconomic fragility, food insecurity, ill health, and mental anguish.

Not contained within national borders, these crises had regional and global consequences. Although the majority of people displaced during the early 2000s remained within their own countries, millions migrated across borders as refugees and asylum-seekers. Most went to neighboring countries. Syrian refugees, for example, migrated mainly into Turkey, Lebanon, Jordan, Egypt, and Iraq, while Venezuelans primarily left for Colombia, Ecuador, Peru, and Brazil. Some attempted to go further, undertaking long and perilous journeys to seek safety and rebuild their lives. Between 2014 and 2021, roughly two million people from Middle Eastern and North African countries attempted to reach Europe by crossing the Mediterranean Sea. These numbers peaked in 2015, with more than one million attempted crossings in that year alone. Between 2016 and 2021, another 1.8 million Honduran, Guatemalan, and Salvadoran migrants tried to reach the United States, most of them traveling through Mexico on foot toward the US-Mexico border.

These patterns of long-term displacement and migration presented myriad humanitarian challenges. Already fleeing situations of extreme violence, refugees and asylum-seekers faced new forms of danger. During the 2010s, more than twenty-thousand people drowned or disappeared while attempting to cross the Mediterranean. Thousands more died on the arduous overland journey through Mexico or while attempting to cross the US border. Those who survived often spent months or years living in refugee camps, detention centers, or shoddily constructed

settlements, subjected to dismal conditions and abuse. As large
numbers of migrants arrived in other nations, they also generated
requirements for food, housing, and other social services. Yet many
of the countries hosting refugees were low-income nations, which
struggled to absorb the financial costs. In wealthier European
countries and the United States, migration became a divisive
political issue, pitting nativist forces and national security concerns
against notions of international humanitarian responsibility.

Adding to the immense suffering that armed violence produced,
natural hazards generated considerable humanitarian need.
Between 2000 and 2020, the UN Office for Disaster Risk
Reduction recorded 7,348 major disaster events—an average of
one just about every day. Cumulatively, these crises claimed
1.23 million lives and affected four billion people in some way.
They also revealed the stubborn challenges of conducting effective
humanitarian responses to disasters, and of preventing them in
the first place.

One of the first major catastrophes of the new millennium
commenced on December 26, 2004, when a series of colossal
tsunami waves smashed into Indonesia, Sri Lanka, Thailand, and
multiple other countries. The Indian Ocean Tsunami killed
230,000 people and left nearly two million homeless. The disaster
galvanized a massive international response. Valued at $13.5
billion, it involved a comprehensive array of relief, recovery, and
rebuilding projects. Though these efforts provided vital assistance
to disaster survivors, they proved highly chaotic, leading to calls
for improved coordination across the aid sector. The Indian Ocean
Tsunami also underscored the importance of reducing disaster
risk, through such technologies as early-warning systems and
hazard-resistant housing and infrastructure. Despite some
concrete efforts to prepare better for future disasters, a lack of
funding and political will ensured that many people remained
susceptible, especially in lower-income nations.

This continued vulnerability became starkly clear in January 2010, when a powerful earthquake occurred in Haiti, triggering a momentous cataclysm. More than 222,000 people died and another 2.3 million were displaced. The earthquake also crippled medical facilities and other infrastructure throughout the region. Once again, this disaster prompted an extraordinary international response. By 2013, official commitments for relief, recovery, and development assistance exceeded ten billion dollars. Despite the large influx of foreign aid workers and dollars, many observers believed that they only had made the situation worse. Critics complained of disorganized and mismanaged aid, slow progress in rebuilding, and unfulfilled promises from donors. Above all, they faulted international aid agencies for failing to consult local people and civil society organizations, ignoring Haitian needs and expertise while undermining Haitian institutions. For many, the 2010 Haitian earthquake became a metonym for the failures of the international humanitarian system.

Although the Indian Ocean Tsunami and Haitian earthquake ranked as the early twenty-first century's two deadliest catastrophes, climate-related disasters affected far greater numbers of people. In a troubling trend, the years from 2000 to 2020 saw a dramatic rise in these types of events, which now accounted for 90 percent of all major disasters. Among the deadliest climate-related disasters were those triggered by intense tropical storms, like Hurricane Katrina in the United States (2005), Cyclone Nargis in Myanmar (2008), Typhoon Haiyan in the Philippines (2013), and Cyclone Idai in southeast Africa (2019). Floods, however, were even more common, affecting some 1.6 billion people during these two decades. Droughts, wildfires, and extreme heat only added to the devastation. In addition to causing deaths and destruction directly, climate-related disasters fed into other humanitarian emergencies. Impacts like agricultural failures and deaths of livestock, for instance,

10. During the twenty-first century, international responses to wars, disasters, and other humanitarian crises have often achieved considerable good, yet they have also led to negative consequences and criticism. The relief and recovery efforts that followed the 2010 earthquake in Haiti revealed some of the myriad challenges facing the international humanitarian system today.

contributed to food insecurity and famine in many countries, while competition for water and arable land fueled conflict, displacement, and migration.

Though crises like these tend to be categorized as "natural disasters," all were caused, at least in part, by human actions and inaction. Social and political problems like poverty and war made certain countries and communities more vulnerable to environmental hazards than others. Human choices and weak governance created many additional risk factors: overcrowded and substandard housing, inadequate zoning and building codes, a lack of investment in mitigation technologies, and settlement in coastal areas, flood plains, or along fault lines. As the early twenty-first century progressed, the effects of anthropogenic climate change played an ever more central role as well.

Although disaster risk reduction had been a stated priority within the aid community since the 1970s, the growing frequency and severity of disasters during the early 2000s confirmed for many humanitarians the need to do more. In disaster, as in armed conflict, short-term relief was essential, yet insufficient. Complex emergencies demanded comprehensive solutions.

The state of humanitarianism today

Today's humanitarianism is a product of both its distant past and recent events. Erected during the nineteenth and twentieth centuries, much of its organizational and legal architecture remains intact, continuing to structure the contemporary humanitarian order. Its defining principles and best practices, though often up for debate, have similarly deep historical roots. Since the 1990s, however, the aid sector has also changed in marked ways. It has experienced staggering growth, major controversies, and significant reforms, intended to make humanitarianism more professionalized, standardized, and accountable to donors and beneficiaries. In the twenty-first century, humanitarian institutions, norms, and concerns have become integral to global governance, to a degree unparalleled in previous generations. For good and for ill, humanitarianism is an essential force in our modern world.

The current humanitarian system is sprawling and diverse. Its core actors, however, can be grouped into four or five broad categories. The constitutive parts of the International Red Cross and Red Crescent Movement form one central node. The International Committee of the Red Cross (ICRC), founded in 1863, retains its mandate to provide neutral and independent assistance to victims of conflict and armed violence. It also acts as a guardian of international humanitarian law, promoting respect for the Geneva Conventions of 1949 and their Additional Protocols. The League of Red Cross Societies (LRCS), founded in 1919, was renamed the International Federation of Red Cross and

Red Crescent Societies (IFRC) in 1991. It continues to coordinate assistance for disaster survivors, refugees, and those in health emergencies. The IFRC also supports the work of 192 National Red Cross and Red Crescent Societies, which serve as independent humanitarian auxiliaries to governments in almost every country.

A second set of key players comprise the specialized agencies of the UN system. Many UN agencies established during the mid-twentieth century remain crucial fixtures in the humanitarian field today. Chief among them, in terms of funding and programming, are the World Food Programme, the UN High Commissioner for Refugees (UNHCR), and the United Nations Children's Fund. Other key agencies include the World Health Organization, the Food and Agriculture Organization, the UN Development Programme, and the UN Relief and Works Agency for Palestine Refugees. During the 1990s, the UN Secretary-General established an Office for the Coordination of Humanitarian Affairs (OCHA), which continues to operate today. OCHA is charged with orchestrating a coherent international response to disasters, conflicts, and other emergencies. It also performs humanitarian policy and advocacy work.

Nation-states and government agencies form the third pillar of the humanitarian system. The lion's share of humanitarian and development aid spending each year comes from a small handful of wealthy nations. In terms of total expenditures, the US government has for decades ranked as the largest public donor (though at present, this appears to be changing). Other leading contributors include Germany, Japan, France, the United Kingdom, and European Union institutions. When aid spending is measured as a percentage of gross national income (GNI), however, other governments stand out as far more generous. Nordic countries like Sweden, Luxembourg, Norway, and Denmark rank highest, as do several Gulf states, including the United Arab Emirates, Saudi Arabia, and Turkey. For the world's leading donor nations, humanitarian aid remains a critical foreign policy instrument, a means to project soft power, and a tool of nation-branding.

Nongovernmental organizations are the final cornerstone of the contemporary humanitarian sector. Today, an estimated five thousand different voluntary humanitarian organizations exist in the world. Some are faith-based, others secular. Some focus on short-term relief, others on long-term development assistance. Some are based in single countries, while others have dozens of national affiliates. Most of the largest and most influential NGOs operating in the humanitarian field today originated in response to twentieth-century crises. They include Save the Children, Oxfam International, Médecins Sans Frontières, BRAC, World Vision International, the International Rescue Committee, Caritas Internationalis, Islamic Relief, the Danish Refugee Council, CARE International, and the Norwegian Refugee Council. The International Council of Voluntary Agencies, founded in 1962, remains a vital forum for coordinating the work of these and dozens of other organizations.

Some include a fifth node in this system: the private sector. Wealthy philanthropists like Warren Buffett, the Bill & Melinda Gates Foundation, and the David and Lucile Packard Foundation have become major donors to humanitarian causes in recent decades, contributing billions of dollars per year. So have multinational corporations. The IKEA Foundation, for instance, ranks as one of the world's largest philanthropies and supports anti-poverty programs in less-wealthy countries. The e-commerce giant Amazon, meanwhile, has assumed a central role in global disaster relief and response, using its immense logistical capabilities to deliver aid supplies to affected communities. Whether through individual philanthropy or corporate stewardship, the private sector exerts considerable influence on the humanitarian marketplace.

Though its broad outlines have remained relatively consistent over the past few decades, the humanitarian system is by no means static. By almost all measures, it is expanding at a breakneck pace. The number of people employed in humanitarian careers has skyrocketed in recent years. In 2010, an estimated 210,000 people were employed as personnel for major humanitarian agencies. By 2022, that figure had tripled, reaching 630,000. The vast majority, roughly 90 percent, were national staff employed in their own countries. Expenditures have grown at a similarly astronomic rate, transforming the aid sector into a multibillion-dollar industry. In 1995, total public and private funding for international humanitarian assistance was roughly $4.6 billion. By 2012, that figure had risen to $16.4 billion, and by 2022 it reached $46.9 billion—a tenfold increase in less than three decades. The budgets of many NGOs and UN and government agencies have seen similar gains.

Sadly, humanitarian needs are also growing at a rapid clip. In 1995, 18.1 million people were refugees in other countries and another 4.3 million were internally displaced. By 2023, those figures had quintupled, with 114 million people displaced either internally or across borders. In 2024 alone, an estimated 300 million people in seventy-two countries required humanitarian assistance and protection. Despite rising expenditures, mounting needs have far outpaced total aid spending, creating a yawning humanitarian funding gap. In 2023, the gap between requirements and available funds reached a record $32.5 billion shortfall, leaving roughly 60 percent of humanitarian needs unmet. Since that time, the gap has only continued to widen, a trend exacerbated by the US government's decision to slash foreign aid spending in early 2025. What limited resources are available, moreover, are not distributed evenly among crises, meaning that some populations receive far less aid than they require.

Funding shortfalls are not the only difficulties plaguing modern humanitarianism. In recent years, the sector has faced multiple criticisms, challenges, and truly existential threats.

The entrenched power dynamics between aid donors and aid recipients have long underpinned critiques of the humanitarian order, and they remain a chief point of contention today. People affected by crises commonly reproach humanitarian practitioners for failing to treat them with dignity and for excluding them from humanitarian decision-making. Many critics assert that cultural chauvinism and racism, both individual and structural, is pervasive within the sector. They also denounce the dominance that major aid agencies and donor governments, based in the Global North, exercise over crisis-affected communities, overwhelmingly in the Global South. Illustrating this point, even though national staff represent 90 percent of the humanitarian workforce, they are severely underrepresented in the leadership of global aid organizations and paid far less than their international counterparts. The modern aid industry, its critics argue, perpetuates colonial-era political and economic hierarchies. These unequal relationships fuel distrust of humanitarian action, undermining its effectiveness in crisis situations.

Further eroding trust are reports of humanitarians causing direct harm to the populations they serve. Most glaringly, repeated revelations of sexual exploitation and abuse have roiled the aid world in recent years. In 2015, evidence emerged that UN Peacekeepers had sexually assaulted multiple people in the Central African Republic. In 2018, multiple senior officials with Oxfam were exposed for hiring Haitian sex workers following the 2010 earthquake. And in 2019 and 2020, journalists uncovered systematic abuses in Mozambique and the Democratic Republic of Congo, where aid workers routinely traded food or jobs for sex. If these reports were not damning enough, whistleblowers also testified to a culture of impunity within many aid agencies, with leadership covering up abuses and shielding personnel who committed them. For many aid recipients, such allegations cast grave doubts on the aid sector's principled pledge to "do no harm."

Accompanying this external opprobrium, serious concerns have surfaced within the aid community. At the height of the #MeToo movement in the 2010s, for one, many aid workers came forth with allegations of sexual harassment, bullying, inappropriate behavior, and gender discrimination. These reports highlighted a toxic culture within some of the world's most influential humanitarian organizations. Rising violence against aid workers poses another serious worry. Over the past few decades, deliberate attacks on humanitarian personnel have left thousands dead and wounded. In 2022 alone, 444 aid workers were attacked, 116 killed, and 185 kidnapped. Aggressors have also targeted hospitals, aid convoys, and other facilities, crippling humanitarian work in Gaza, South Sudan, Syria, Yemen, and other sites. Aid organizations have experimented with various strategies to decrease these risks, including armored trucks, fortified compounds, or withdrawing from particularly dangerous regions. Such approaches impede humanitarian action, however, while also erecting barriers between aid workers and affected populations. Better solutions are needed to protect both humanitarian personnel and the people they serve.

Further confounding matters, violence against aid workers may be just one symptom of a broader and more nefarious trend, toward what researcher Alex de Waal terms "counter-humanitarianism." Many participants in twenty-first-century crises—including governments, militaries, and nonstate armed groups—are flouting or flat-out rejecting traditional humanitarian norms and laws. Their behaviors display a callous indifference toward human life and a disavowal of the humanitarian principles that developed over the past two centuries. Blockades of food and medicine, deliberate attacks on civilian targets, hostility toward refugees and asylum-seekers, and denial of life-saving assistance are just a few examples of this counter-humanitarian ideology in practice. Though these sorts of actions occurred in earlier generations, some analysts warn they are happening more frequently, suggesting a worrisome backlash against humanitarianism's core values.

Even when belligerents respect international humanitarian law, the changing nature of modern warfare presents innumerable challenges for aid workers operating in today's conflict zones. Though they tend to produce fewer violent deaths than their twentieth-century antecedents, modern armed conflicts regularly devolve into entrenched, systemic emergencies. Humanitarian organizations struggle to address the comprehensive needs of populations affected by these prolonged crises and "forever wars." At the same time, the transition from industrialized to computerized warfare is creating new ethical dilemmas and novel humanitarian concerns. Rather than conscripting large armies and inflicting mass casualties, today's militaries increasingly rely on precision drones and AI systems to attack enemy targets from great distances. Proponents maintain that remote cyberwarfare will reduce battlefield casualties and minimize collateral damage. Critics, however, contend that it dehumanizes enemy combatants and inures drone operators to the fates of civilians caught in the crossfire.

As the climate crisis accelerates, today's humanitarian challenges will only intensify. Future conflicts will be driven by a host of climate-related stressors, including deadly heat, ecosystem collapse, resource competition, emerging disease threats, and the migration of up to one billion people from uninhabitable regions. Even if they do not precipitate armed violence, these pressures will cause immense and prolonged suffering, giving rise to many nonconflict emergencies. "Climate change is an existential threat to humanity," the Secretary General of the IFRC recently warned, "and the entire humanitarian sector needs to take it very seriously."

Although these apocalyptic scenarios might appear to suggest otherwise, contemporary humanitarianism is not all doom and gloom. The crises facing the aid sector have also spurred reform movements and some hopeful changes, intended to improve humanitarian action today and in the century ahead.

For one, the aid sector has seen a concerted push to develop industry-wide standards and professional codes of conduct. An early move in this direction came in 1997, when a group of leading humanitarian agencies launched the Sphere movement. They drafted a *Humanitarian Charter*, outlining the rights, obligations, and principles that all humanitarian actors must respect. They also produced the *Sphere Handbook*, an internationally recognized set of minimum standards for aid practitioners. Revised and updated in the decades since, both documents remain widely influential. More recently, during the first World Humanitarian Summit of 2016, major humanitarian donors and aid organizations unveiled an initiative called the "Grand Bargain." This agreement comprises fifty-one shared commitments, intended to improve the efficacy, quality, and efficiency of humanitarian response. At its most fundamental level, its goal is to get more aid into the hands of people who truly need it.

Accompanying the development of these professional standards were simultaneous demands for greater accountability across the humanitarian sector. Twenty-first-century aid agencies are expected to be accountable to their funders, demonstrating quantifiable evidence of their impacts through reporting, evaluations, and metrics. More recently, the emphasis has shifted from donors to beneficiaries, and to holding aid workers accountable to the populations they serve. Achieving this goal requires incorporating local needs and desires into humanitarian decision-making and remaining open and responsive to feedback and grievances. Additionally, it demands taking action against practitioners who fail to uphold core principles and minimum standards.

Reformers have also advanced more radical proposals to "decolonize" and "localize" aid. Though they are not fully synonymous, these intertwined movements share many similar assumptions and goals. Calls for decolonizing aid begin with the premise that the international humanitarian system is a historical legacy of Western imperialism. In its current form, this system preserves deep-rooted power imbalances between aid recipients and wealthy donor nations and agencies. It also privileges humanitarian approaches and philosophies that originated in the Global North, presenting them as superior and universal. Proponents of decolonizing aid demand a fundamental restructuring of the existing humanitarian order. They seek to shift resources and influence toward affected populations, ensuring that they play a central role in humanitarian governance. They also celebrate the value of non-Western traditions and practices, promoting a more diverse and capacious understanding of humanitarianism.

Proponents of localizing aid prioritize the equitable inclusion and participation of actors in places affected by crisis, acknowledging that people on the ground already provide the lion's share of humanitarian assistance in their communities. International aid, they argue, should focus on supporting the capabilities of ordinary people and strengthening local and national institutions. It should build community resilience to climate shocks, natural hazards, and other threats, enabling societies to cope with, adapt to, and recover from crises without outside assistance. Emphasizing the human dignity of aid beneficiaries, supporters of localization seek to empower these individuals to assert their rights and participate fully in humanitarian decision-making. One concrete example of this approach, which has become increasingly influential in recent years, is to give aid recipients direct cash transfers rather than in-kind aid. This form of humanitarian assistance enables people to decide what sort of aid they need (and prefer) while also supporting local economies and markets. Advocates consider cash transfers a more sustainable, just, and dignified form of aid.

Localization, decolonization, standardization, and accountability have all become part of the current humanitarian vernacular. More than just buzzwords, these objectives represent central priorities across the contemporary aid sector. Whether the impact of these reforms will be real and transformative, or merely rhetorical, remains to be seen.

Despite ongoing efforts to improve humanitarianism, people around the world continue to suffer in armed conflicts, disasters, and other humanitarian emergencies. As I complete this book in early 2025, major crises are gripping Afghanistan, Burkina Faso, the Democratic Republic of Congo, Ethiopia, Gaza/Israel, Haiti, Myanmar, Niger, Somalia, South Sudan, Sudan, Syria, Ukraine, Venezuela, and Yemen. In these places—and in far too many others—hundreds of millions of people are experiencing extreme hunger, displacement, and life-threatening violence. Humanitarian needs are growing yet increasingly going unmet. Drivers of humanitarian crises are evolving, seemingly faster than the aid sector can adapt.

What can we do?

Humanitarianism is a human creation, a system of values and principles built by many societies and cultures over centuries. It has always been imperfect, and it is hardly beyond reproach. Yet its essential aim, at least in its ideal form, is an admirable one: to make things better for humanity in an inhumane world. Looking ahead, it is urgent for a new generation of humanitarians to continue working toward that goal, striving to improve the aid sector and the spaces in which it operates. But all of us can play a part, too. Understanding humanitarianism's history, with all its ethical contradictions and complexities, can help us determine how to do better—or how to do our best—amid current and future crises. We can embrace the essential principle that humanity is universal and shared by all people, while also celebrating the rich diversity of global humanitarian traditions. Both are possible at once. In the face of crisis, we can refuse to succumb to indifference or inertia. We can commit to saving lives, alleviating suffering, respecting human dignity, and maintaining compassion and empathy toward one another.

References

Chapter 1: What is humanitarianism?

United Nations General Assembly, *One Humanity, Shared Responsibility: Report of the Secretary-General for the World Humanitarian Summit*, A/70/709 (January 31, 2016), undocs.org/en/A/70/709.

Statutes of the International Red Cross and Red Crescent Movement (adopted October 1986; amended December 1995 and June 2006), icrc.org/en/doc/assets/files/other/statutes-en-a5.pdf.

David Rieff, *A Bed for the Night: Humanitarianism in Crisis* (Simon & Schuster, 2002).

Michael Barnett, *Empire of Humanity: A History of Humanitarianism* (Cornell University Press, 2011), 21.

Leo Tolstoy, quoted in "Tolstoi Writes of War: Says It Must Follow Slavery and Disappear," *New York Times* (January 17, 1897), 15, referenced in Samuel Moyn, *Humane: How the United States Abandoned Peace and Reinvented War* (Farrar, Straus and Giroux, 2021), 38.

Michael Geyer, "Humanitarianism and Human Rights: A Troubled Rapport," in *The Emergence of Humanitarian Intervention: Ideas and Practice from the Nineteenth Century to the Present*, ed. Fabian Klose (Cambridge University Press, 2016), 31.

Emily Baughan, "History and Humanitarianism: A Conversation," *Past and Present* 241 (November 2018): e18.

Chapter 2: Origin stories

John Calhoun, speaking in 12th Cong., 1st sess., *Annals of Congress* (April 29, 1812): 1348.

Frederick Douglass, "The Meaning of July Fourth for the Negro," speech, July 5, 1852, published in *Frederick Douglass: Selected Speeches and Writings*, ed. Philip S. Foner (Lawrence Hill, 1999), 188–206.

Andrew Jackson, "First Annual Message to Congress," in *A Compilation of the Messages and Papers of the Presidents*, ed. James D. Richardson (Bureau of National Literature, 1897), 1021.

Davide Rodogno, *Against Massacre: Humanitarian Interventions in the Ottoman Empire* (Princeton University Press, 2012), 88.

Fabian Klose, *In the Cause of Humanity: A History of Humanitarian Intervention in the Long Nineteenth Century* (Cambridge University Press, 2022), 147.

Tania Ixchel Atilano, "The 1871 Mexican Criminal Code as the Missing Piece in the History of Criminalizing Violations of the Laws of War," *International Review of the Red Cross* 920–921 (November 2022): 1660.

Chapter 3: Organizational and legal structures

Caroline Moorhead, *Dunant's Dream: War, Switzerland and the History of the Red Cross* (Carroll & Graf, 1999).

John F. Hutchinson, *Champions of Charity: War and the Rise of the Dred Cross* (Westview Press, 1996), 103.

Convention (II) with Respect to the Laws and Customs of War on Land, preamble (July 29, 1899), ihl-databases.icrc.org/en/ihl-treaties/hague-conv-ii-1899.

W. E. B. Du Bois, "To the Nations of the World" (1900), reprinted *W. E. B. Du Bois: International Thought*, ed. Adom Getachew and Jennifer Pitts (Cambridge University Press, 2022), 20.

Fabian Klose, *In the Cause of Humanity: A History of Humanitarian Intervention in the Long Nineteenth Century* (Cambridge University Press, 2022), 233.

International Committee of the Red Cross, appeal to the belligerents, February 8, 1918, https://www.icrc.org/en/doc/resources/documents/statement/57jnqh.htm.

Daniel Maul, "The Rise of a Humanitarian Superpower: American NGOs and International Relief, 1917–1945," in *Internationalism,*

Imperialism, and the Formation of the Contemporary World: The Pasts of the Present, ed. M. B. Jerónimo and J. P. Monteiro (Palgrave Macmillan, 2018), 127–46.

Chapter 4: From one world war to another

H. G. Wells, *The War That Will End War* (Frank & Cecil Palmer, 1914).

Herbert Hoover to Woodrow Wilson, October 1919, Box 20, Pre-Commerce Papers, Herbert Hoover Papers, Herbert Hoover Presidential Library, West Branch, Iowa.

Emily Baughan, *Saving the Children: Humanitarianism, Internationalism, and Empire* (University of California Press, 2022), 27.

Convention et Statuts Établissant une Union Internationale de Secours, July 12, 1927, P-UIS F 2-34, records of l'Union Internationale de Secours, Archives of the International Committee of the Red Cross, Geneva, Switzerland.

Dame Rachel Crowdy, "The Humanitarian Activities of the League of Nations," address on April 12, 1927, *Journal of the Royal Institute of International Affairs* 6, no. 3 (May 1927): 153.

Geneva Declaration of the Rights of the Child, adopted September 26, 1924, http://un-documents.net/gdrc1924.htm.

Arthur W. Dunn, "Education for World Understanding Through the Junior Red Cross," *Progressive Education* 18 (Spring 1925): 88–91.

"Fiftieth Anniversary of the Liberation of Auschwitz Concentration Camp," *International Review of the Red Cross* 35, no. 304 (1995): 109–10.

United Nations Convention on the Prevention and Punishment of the Crime of Genocide, December 9, 1948, 78 U.N.T.S. 276 (entered into force January 12, 1951), https://treaties.un.org/doc/publication/unts/volume%2078/volume-78-i-1021-english.pdf.

Chapter 5: Cold wars, hot wars, decolonization, and development

UN General Assembly Resolution 2198 (XXI), "Protocol Relating to the Status of Refugees," December 16, 1966, https://www.ohchr.org/en/instruments-mechanisms/instruments/protocol-relating-status-refugees.

UN General Assembly Resolution A/RES/1219 (XII), "Financing of
Economic Development," December 14, 1957, http://undocs.org/
en/A/RES/1219(XII).

XXth International Conference of the Red Cross, "Proclamation of the
Fundamental Principles of the Red Cross," October 29, 1965,
https://www.icrc.org/en/doc/resources/documents/misc/
fundamental-principles-commentary-010179.htm.

Lyndon B. Johnson to E. Palmer Hoy, March 4, 1965, Folder FO 3-2,
Box 47, Confidential File, White House Central Files,
Lyndon B. Johnson Presidential Library, Austin, Texas.

Memorandum handed to the Chairman of the European Council, June
2, 1971, quoted in Kevin O'Sullivan, *The NGO Moment: The
Globalisation of Compassion from Biafra to Live Aid* (Cambridge
University Press, 2021), 39.

Band Aid, "Do They Know It's Christmas," recorded November 1984,
Sarm West Studios, UK.

Chapter 6: Humanitarianism in flux

George W. Bush, address before a joint session of the Congress on the
State of the Union, January 29, 1991, https://bush41library.tamu.
edu/archives/public-papers/2656.

Mary Kaldor, *New and Old Wars: Organized Violence in a Global Era*
(Polity Press, 1999).

Fiona Fox, "New Humanitarianism: Does It Provide a Moral Banner
for the 21st Century?" *Disasters* 25, no. 4 (2001): 275–89.

Kofi Annan, " 'We the Peoples': The Role of the United Nations in the
21st century" (UN Department of Public Information, 2000),
https://digitallibrary.un.org/record/413745?ln=en&v=pdf.

UN Office for the Coordination of Humanitarian Affairs, "Afghanistan:
Humanitarian Update, May 2023," June 15, 2023, https://reliefweb.
int/report/afghanistan/afghanistan-humanitarian-update-
may-2023.

Colin L. Powell, remarks to the National Foreign Policy Conference
for Leaders of Nongovernmental Organizations, October 26, 2001,
https://avalon.law.yale.edu/sept11/powell_brief31.asp.

Ban Ki-moon, "Renewal, Not Restoration, Should Be the Goal for
Haiti," *Washington Post*, March 29, 2010, https://www.un.org/sg/
en/content/sg/articles/2010-03-29/renewal-not-restoration-
should-be-goal-haiti.

Alex de Waal, *Mass Starvation: The History and Future of Famine* (Polity Press, 2018), 196–98.

Jagan Chapagain, news release, June 22, 2021, https://www.icrc.org/en/document/red-cross-red-crescent-humanitarian-sector-joins-forces-tackle-existential-threat-climate.

Further reading

Allen, Tim, Anna MacDonald, and Henry Radice, eds.
  Humanitarianism: A Dictionary of Concepts. Routledge, 2018.
Barnett, Michael N. *Empire of Humanity: A History of
  Humanitarianism.* Cornell University Press, 2013.
Barnett, Michael N., ed. *Humanitarianism and Human Rights:
  A World of Differences?* Cambridge University Press, 2020.
Baughan, Emily. *Saving the Children: Humanitarianism,
  Internationalism, and Empire.* University of California
  Press, 2021.
Crossland, James. *War, Law and Humanity: The Campaign to Control
  Warfare, 1853–1914.* Bloomsbury Academic, 2018.
Davey, Eleanor. *Idealism Beyond Borders: The French Revolutionary
  Left and the Rise of Humanitarianism, 1954–1988.* Cambridge
  University Press, 2015.
de Waal, Alex. *Mass Starvation: The History and Future of Famine.*
  Polity Press, 2018.
Dijk, Boyd van. *Preparing for War: The Making of the Geneva
  Conventions.* Oxford University Press, 2022.
Everill, Bronwen, and Josiah David Kaplan, eds. *The History and
  Practice of Humanitarian Intervention and Aid in Africa.* Palgrave
  Macmillan, 2013.
Fassin, Didier. *Humanitarian Reason: A Moral History of the Present
  Times.* University of California Press, 2012.
Fassin, Didier, and Mariella Pandolfi, eds. *Contemporary States of
  Emergency: The Politics of Military and Humanitarian
  Interventions.* Zone Books, 2010.

Feldman, Ilana. *Life Lived in Relief: Humanitarian Predicaments and Palestinian Refugee Politics.* University of California Press, 2018.

Feldman, Ilana, and Miriam Iris Ticktin, eds. *In the Name of Humanity: The Government of Threat and Care.* Duke University Press, 2010.

Fiori, Juliano, Fernando Espada, Andrea Rigon, Bertrand Taithe, and Rafia Zakaria, eds. *Amidst the Debris: Humanitarianism and the End of Liberal Order.* Hurst & Company, 2021.

Forsythe, David P. *The Contemporary International Committee of the Red Cross: Challenges, Changes, Controversies.* Cambridge University Press, 2024.

Forsythe, David P. *The Humanitarians: The International Committee of the Red Cross.* Cambridge University Press, 2005.

Fuller, Pierre. *Famine Relief in Warlord China.* Harvard University Press, 2019.

Glasman, Joël. *Humanitarianism and the Quantification of Human Needs: Minimal Humanity.* Routledge, 2020.

Hong, Young-Sun. *Cold War Germany, the Third World, and the Global Humanitarian Regime.* Cambridge University Press, 2015.

Hutchinson, John F. *Champions of Charity: War and the Rise of the Red Cross.* Westview Press, 1996.

Klose, Fabian, ed. *The Emergence of Humanitarian Intervention: Ideas and Practice from the Nineteenth Century to the Present.* Cambridge University Press, 2016.

Klose, Fabian. *In the Cause of Humanity: A History of Humanitarian Intervention in the Long Nineteenth Century.* Cambridge University Press, 2022.

Lester, Alan, and Fae Dussart. *Colonization and the Origins of Humanitarian Governance: Protecting Aborigines Across the Nineteenth-Century British Empire.* Cambridge University Press, 2014.

Malkki, Liisa H. *The Need to Help: The Domestic Arts of International Humanitarianism.* Duke University Press, 2015.

Mantilla, Giovanni. *Lawmaking Under Pressure: International Humanitarian Law and Internal Armed Conflict.* Cornell University Press, 2020.

Moyn, Samuel. *Humane: How the United States Abandoned Peace and Reinvented War.* Farrar, Straus and Giroux, 2021.

Ó Gráda, Cormac. *Famine: A Short History.* Princeton University Press, 2009.

O'Sullivan, Kevin. *The NGO Moment: The Globalisation of Compassion from Biafra to Live Aid.* Cambridge University Press, 2021.

Paulmann, Johannes, ed. *Dilemmas of Humanitarian Aid in the Twentieth Century.* Oxford University Press, 2016.

Piller, Elisabeth, and Neville Wylie, eds. *Humanitarianism and the Greater War, 1914–24.* Manchester University Press, 2023.

Proctor, Tammy M. *Saving Europe: First World War Relief and American Identity.* Oxford University Press, 2025.

Ramalingam, Ben. *Aid on the Edge of Chaos: Rethinking International Cooperation in a Complex World.* Oxford University Press, 2014.

Rodogno, Davide. *Against Massacre: Humanitarian Interventions in the Ottoman Empire, 1815–1914.* Princeton University Press, 2011.

Rodogno, Davide. *Night on Earth: A History of International Humanitarianism in the Near East, 1918–1930.* Cambridge University Press, 2022.

Rossi, Benedetta. *From Slavery to Aid: Politics, Labour, and Ecology in the Nigerien Sahel, 1800–2000.* Cambridge University Press, 2017.

Salvatici, Silvia. *A History of Humanitarianism, 1755–1989: In the Name of Others.* Manchester University Press, 2019.

Sasson, Tehila. *The Solidarity Economy: Nonprofits and the Making of Neoliberalism After Empire.* Princeton University Press, 2024.

Scott-Smith, Tom. *On an Empty Stomach: Two Hundred Years of Hunger Relief.* Cornell University Press, 2020.

Slim, Hugo. *Humanitarian Ethics: A Guide to the Morality of Aid in War and Disaster.* Oxford University Press, 2015.

Slim, Hugo. *Solferino 21: Warfare, Civilians and Humanitarians in the Twenty-First Century.* Hurst & Company, 2022.

Sobocinska, Agnieszka. *Saving the World? Western Volunteers and the Rise of the Humanitarian-Development Complex.* Cambridge University Press, 2021.

Tanielian, Melanie S. *The Charity of War: Famine, Humanitarian Aid, and World War I in the Middle East.* Stanford University Press, 2017.

Teitel, Ruti G. *Humanity's Law.* Oxford University Press, 2011.

Ticktin, Miriam Iris. *Casualties of Care: Immigration and the Politics of Humanitarianism in France.* University of California Press, 2011.

Tudor, Margot. *Blue Helmet Bureaucrats: United Nations Peacekeeping and the Reinvention of Colonialism, 1945–1971.* Cambridge University Press, 2023.

Tusan, Michelle Elizabeth, ed. *Smyrnas Ashes: Humanitarianism, Genocide, and the Birth of the Middle East.* University of California Press, 2012.

Walker, Peter, and Daniel G. Maxwell. *Shaping the Humanitarian World.* Routledge, 2009.

Weiss, Thomas G. *Humanitarian Business.* Polity Press, 2013.

Wylie, Neville, Melanie Oppenheimer, and James Crossland, eds. *The Red Cross Movement: Myths, Practices and Turning Points.* Manchester University Press, 2020.

Index

For the benefit of digital users, indexed terms that span two pages (e.g., 52–53) may, on occasion, appear on only one of those pages.